ORGANIZING
SPECIAL EVENTS
AND CONFERENCES

This revision makes it even easier for you to find the help you need to plan, coordinate, and produce special events. The Resources section on pages 120–125 has been updated to include website information and e-mail addresses, saving you time and money in the planning stages.

ORGANIZING
SPECIAL EVENTS
AND CONFERENCES

A Practical Guide for Busy Volunteers and Staff

Revised Edition

Darcy Campion Devney

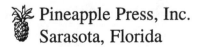 Pineapple Press, Inc.
Sarasota, Florida

Inquiries should be addressed to:

Pineapple Press, Inc.
P.O. Box 3889
Sarasota, Florida 34230

www.pineapplepress.com

Library of Congress Cataloging in Publication Data

Devney, Darcy Campion, 1960–
   Organizing special events and conferences : a practical guide for busy volunteers and staff / Darcy Campion Devney.— revised ed.
      p.   cm.
   Includes bibliographical references and index.
   ISBN 1-56164-217-7 (alk. paper)
1. Special events—Handbooks, manuals, etc. 2. Meetings—Handbooks, manuals, etc. I. Title.

GT3405.D47 2001
394.2'068—dc21

                                                                                00-045313

First Edition
10 9 8 7 6 5 4 3 2

Design by Joan Lange Kresek

ACKNOWLEDGMENTS

I am grateful to all the people who gave me advice, interviews, and examples for this publication. Staff members of more than fifty convention and visitors bureaus and chambers of commerce were most helpful.

Busy event managers, paid and volunteer, were invaluable resources for me. I must mention Alice Freer, of Alice Freer Special Events, and Marion Denby, of The Planned Event, who were both very encouraging. And Shelley Sommer was chock-full of funny stories. I would like to thank the members of House Skold and Marian Walke, who taught me how to be an event manager before I knew any written resources existed.

Special thanks go to Cassandra Boell, who took my rough ideas, added creativity and style, and produced clever, professional illustrations, and to Jo-Ann MacElhiney, whose meticulous index makes the book easy to use.

My family was right behind me all the way, to make sure that the first book by a Devney was published. My husband, Robert Kuhn, gave extraordinary support and encouragement. My brother, Robert Devney, Jr., was a terrific editor and gave freely of his time (again, and again, and again). This book is my thanks, I hope.

And, of course, a special thanks to David Cussen, who knew what I was talking about and thought other people would read it.

CONTENTS

LIST OF GRAPHICS

INTRODUCTION

As one volunteer put it, after working for three years on organizing an international academic convention: "It would have been nice to have known some of the potential hazards in advance—it would have been nice to know a whole lot of things."

There are nearly one million nonprofit organizations in the United States. Every one of them depends for its very survival on one particular functionary: the event manager. Without event managers, there would be no fundraising, no conventions, no new members, no annual celebrations—none of the events which keep an organization going.

Is This Book for You?

You may feel a kinship with these people, who wrote to an advice column for help:

"Our parent-teacher organization is currently making plans for next year's fundraiser. I would really appreciate it if those of you who are involved in this type of organization would share your ideas . . . "

"The women's club of my church is organizing a mother- daughter banquet . . . I would like suggestions for games, contests (such as most-look-alike), entertainment for all ages, decorations, music."

"My high school class is having a 35th reunion. We are in the process of planning it and would like some ideas for prizes, awards, perhaps suggestions to get more of the classmates to participate on our big night. If any of you can give us the benefit of your experience, what works and what doesn't, it would be greatly appreciated."

"I have a new Brownie troop and together with some other troops we would like to arrange a special night to spotlight career women. I want to get a panel of interesting women willing to talk to the girls about their careers, and answer questions from the girls and their moms. I'm interested in any suggestions . . ."

"If any of you has had experience with block parties, could you help me out? I'd like to know what time of year to have it, how to invite people, what to serve, how to introduce people, how it turned out for you, and if you felt more comfortable in your neighborhood afterwards."

Or you may be concerned with just one area of an event, as Mauri Edwards, a professional event planner, hypothesizes in *Successful Meetings*: "Do you know how to trim a speech that's listless and too long and turn it into something worth listening to? How do you keep various speakers' speeches from overlapping or contradicting each other? How do you vary that mass of meeting material by using stage devices sometimes rather than speeches? How do you pace your show? . . . "

Most event managers learn as I did: from listening to more experienced members of their organizations, and by the seat of their pants. There's never been a textbook for special events management. There are some professional associations which concentrate on special events and meeting management; unfortunately, they do not acknowledge the vast number of volunteers working on special events and conferences—and most do not allow them membership.

So I decided to write this book to help busy volunteers and staff produce special events. I started thinking about my own experiences organizing events for nonprofit organizations, both as a volunteer and as a staff member. Then I talked to volunteers and paid staff about their organizations and their events. I interviewed managers of events which attract 100 people and events which attract 100,000 people. I collected samples from events near and far. I read trade publications like *Successful Meetings* and *Fundraising Management* and attended seminars taught by professional meeting managers. And I searched for nuggets of advice in books on parties, hospitality management, public relations, personnel management, graphic arts, facilities management, and catering.

The result is this book, a hands-on guide to organizing any kind of special event or conference. "Hands-on" means you'll find checklists, schedules, models, and examples throughout the book that you can apply in organizing your own particular event.

A Brief Outline

Part One is a broad overview of your job as event manager and includes information on creating the event, assembling your staff, and evaluating the entire experience.

Part Two focuses on the nuts-and-bolts aspects of budget and site, covering ticket pricing, financial sponsors, tax rulings, choosing a location, setting up a site, insurance and security considerations, and cleaning up after the event.

Part Three shows you what other people see: publicity, media relations, and registration. This section will help you design posters, write press releases, keep track of reservations, and set up an admissions checkpoint.

Part Four helps you select and schedule your event programming and contains a sampling of activities and entertainments.

Part Five deals with food and includes chapters on menu planning, quantity shopping and cooking, and quality presentation and serving.

There's also a resource appendix of publications and organizations that you may find helpful for your particular event.

How to Use This Book

This book is, of course, a guide, not a rule book. Every event is a reflection of its own manager.

Organizing Special Events and Conferences is arranged by broad areas of responsibility. As the event manager, you share all the planning and decisions for your event. Use the schedules and job descriptions provided at the beginning of relevant chapters to check on your workers and their progress. Ideally, each person should read the chapters that discuss his or her area of responsibility.

As you read through this book, flag all the points that will apply particularly to your event. Don't be afraid to mark up this book (unless you borrowed this copy from the library—if so, photocopy the worksheets and schedules you need). Use this book as a workbook.

Wherever possible, I have used and explained the professional terms of the specific field. Many volunteers or clerical staff who work on special events eventually transfer their experience to paid professional jobs—as caterers, public relations practitioners, meeting managers, and so on. This transition is usually successful; I hope it will be easier if you already know the "buzz words" of the business.

An Important Note

This guide emphasizes all the work involved in event planning, but much of that work can be fun. Try not to lose sight of that when you're up to your elbows in mailing labels, or think you might not have charged enough per person and are wondering where the extra money will come from. Keep your sense of humor, and remember that your efforts make the event possible. Managers are catalysts; by adding a cup of creativity and a gallon of patience, you help to create a feast for all our senses.

1. EVENT SCHEDULE

Timing	Task
5-12 months prior to event	■ Recruit and meet with committee. ■ Meet with chapter president. ■ Decide purpose of event. ■ Outline audience characteristics. ■ Brainstorm event theme. ■ Select and confirm site and price. ■ Declare event name, date, and theme. ■ Invite exhibitors and vendors.
3-5 months prior	■ Meet monthly with chapter president. ■ Meet monthly with committee. ■ Figure preliminary budget with treasurer. ■ Choose caterer; draft menu. ■ Outline schedule and program. ■ Draw master site diagram. ■ Apply for permits, licenses, etc. ■ Contact entertainers and speakers. ■ Send publicity to newsletters.
2-3 months prior	■ Meet monthly with chapter president. ■ Meet monthly with committee. ■ Print and send invitations. ■ Select performers and entertainers. ■ Mail publicity to external media. ■ Send program to printer.
1-2 months prior	■ Meet monthly with chapter president. ■ Meet monthly with committee. ■ Attend official meetings and events. ■ Collect reservations. ■ Finish final stages of menu planning. ■ Prepare "tasting."
1 month prior	■ Meet with chapter president and all crew managers; walk through site. ■ Confirm all arrangements and contracts. ■ Rehearse speakers and entertainers. ■ Collect items from storage. ■ Make signs. ■ Collate registration packets. ■ Purchase prizes, paper goods, decorations.
2 weeks prior	■ Meet with committee. ■ Call people who were too busy to be crew managers but who might spend some time working at the event.

1. EVENT SCHEDULE (cont'.)

Timing	Task
1 week prior	■ Meet with chapter president. ■ Meet with committee. ■ Close reservation list; type up master. ■ Arrange table and seat allocations. ■ Give final head count to caterer. ■ Print and alphabetize name tags. ■ Deposit last of reservation fees. ■ Order food items. ■ Purchase nonperishable items. ■ Borrow cooking and serving equipment.
1 day prior	■ Purchase perishable foodstuffs. ■ Use checklists to organize and pack. ■ Deliver ingredients to advance cooks. ■ Pick up keys; transport items to the site. ■ Call all crew managers to confirm. ■ Get some sleep (well, at least try).
EVENT DAY	■ Put up directional signs en route. ■ Meet with site officials. ■ Unpack all equipment. ■ Set up registration table. ■ Begin cooking. ■ Open event officially. ■ Begin scheduled activities. ■ Informally interview guests. ■ Set tables and serve refreshments. ■ End of scheduled activities. ■ Clean up kitchen and hall. ■ Reset all furniture. ■ Pack up supplies. ■ Check entire site for lost people and items. ■ Sign out with site officials. ■ Turn out lights; lock up.
1 day after	■ Take down all outdoor signs. ■ Thank all of your volunteers. ■ Clean and return all borrowed items. ■ Return nonperishables to storage. ■ Make notes on event evaluation. ■ Rest and recover.
2-4 weeks after	■ Meet with committee for comment session. ■ Implement evaluation techniques. ■ Finish all budget paperwork. ■ Calculate profit or loss. ■ Write manager's report. ■ Formally submit report to chapter president. ■ Gird your loins for next time.

Chapter 1

AN EVENT MANAGER'S JOB DESCRIPTION

"You don't need to know how the audio in the hall works; you need to know who to ask, who to call. Above all, a good event person is a good manager," declares Shelley Sommer, who has produced events for the Democratic Governors' Association and the John F. Kennedy Presidential Library and Museum.

You may be in charge of an annual meeting, a trade association conference, a political issue seminar, a church bazaar, a neighborhood block party, or a fund-raising costume ball and banquet. Your title may be program organizer, director of special events, meeting manager, company party planner, banquet chairperson, functions planner, seminar leader—or you may claim no title but bear all the responsibility. Although specifics may vary, your job is to act as the manager of a special event or conference for a nonprofit organization.

A Multifaceted Role

An event manager is a person of vision, energy, and commitment in a position of responsibility and authority. (Sometimes, managers even have fun!) An event manager plays myriad professional roles.

After your first few rounds as an event manager, you will probably find that one aspect of the job particularly appeals to you. One of the event managers featured in this book, for example, really enjoys planning menus; another likes the challenge of finding exciting

---

An Event Manager Is a . . .

- Project director: set and define goals; schedule and assign tasks.
- Personnel supervisor: choose, motivate, and evaluate staff.
- Art director: design theme, decorations, and printed materials.
- Executive: evaluate long-term results and make decisions.
- Accountant: plan budget and balance the books.
- Facilities expert: find and use a site to its fullest potential.
- Public relations practitioner: target audience and develop publicity campaign.
- Salesperson: sell the event to the organization, financial sponsors, and the public.
- Box-office consultant: monitor ticket sales and registration process.
- Program administrator: develop and schedule programming.
- Caterer: create nutritious menus and oversee food preparation.
- Captain: choose and implement food service system.

---

new seminar programs. Feel free to delegate every aspect of the event except the area that you really enjoy.

Resources

Draw upon as many resources as you can when you begin planning. You can weed out inappropriate ideas and suggestions later. This book should help you plan and structure your event, and additional references are listed in the resource appendix. Other excellent sources of inspiration and advice are reports from past events.

People Experienced managers can be good mentors, if you feel a bit shaky at first. If you're repeating a previous event, be sure to talk to that event's manager (maybe you think the event was badly run, but you *can* learn from those mistakes). Keep alert at every event and meeting you attend and apply good ideas you discover to your own organization. Also, nearly everyone attends some special events, and attendees can regale you with tales of the best—and worst—events they've attended and why they think so.

Organizations Local organizations should ask for as much help and guidance as possible from their national headquarters. The U.S. Cycling Federation, for example, gives permits and handles insurance coverage, issues licenses, sanctions races for competitive purposes, and recommends judges for cycle clubs across the country. A variety of organizations exist specifically to help nonprofits (such as Retired Senior Volunteer Program, Arts and Business Council, the Independent Sector, and many others). And professional organizations, like the Public Relations Society of America, can often lend an expert to guide an inexperienced volunteer through a specific project. (See Resources.)

Consider combining forces with another group to stage a major event too big for either group to accomplish alone. For example, the Midget Ocean Racing Club sponsors the annual Lake Huron International Regatta, a 160-mile sailboat race. The event draws competitors from Ontario and Michigan; proceeds benefit the Canadian and American Diabetes Associations. Or, perhaps the school band needs the experience of performing and you need an opening act. Try a reverse fundraiser: your group gets the publicity, your partner group gets the profits.

If you are doing an ethnic or international event, enlist the aid of consulates and trade commissions (Houston, for example, has more than thirty consulate generals in residence). Overseas, tourist boards can explain customs, suggest vendors, and translate intricacies. Convention and visitors bureaus in large cities and chambers of commerce in smaller towns can provide a variety of services, often at no charge.

Basic Materials In order to manage an event properly, you will need access to the following items: a telephone (an answering machine is a very useful adjunct); a car; a photocopier; a typewriter (a personal computer is even better); a bank account (or an official organization account). The larger and more complex your event will be, the more important these resources will be in your planning and management.

Personality ("Am I Sure About This?")

You should realistically assess your personality before committing to an event. Are you able to present a calm, friendly, and courteous manner at all times? Alicia Rodriguez is president of Meeting Management Resources, a consulting and seminar business in Wellesley, Massachusetts. She lists five essential characteristics of successful event managers:

- Detail-oriented
- Organized
- Full of energy, both physical and emotional
- Nurturing
- Flexible

And she emphasizes, "Having a good sense of humor is key!"

Motivation Many volunteer event managers confess candidly that they decided to manage a conference or event after attending one that they felt was badly managed; a voice inside said, "Even I could do better than *this*!"

The job of event manager requires hard work and a service orientation; it is not a good position for a glory seeker. The person who wants to sit at the head table, give orders, and look important has the wrong idea of an event manager's function. Some friendly advice from the initiated: "It's going to be more work than you ever anticipated" and "The event is simply not as much fun for the coordinator as for the participants."

Lifestyle Examine your lifestyle and schedule. It may not be a good time for you to manage an event. Here are nine reasons to say "no":

- You're in the throes of a deep personal crisis.
- You're adjusting to a new job or living space.

- You'll be out of town for a few weeks before the event.
- You're the sort of person who quickly loses interest in projects or never finishes anything.
- Your spouse or significant other is feeling ignored.
- You're not a good decision-maker, or you detest compromise.
- You know that large crowds or constant interruptions make you jumpy.
- You have other important commitments—a final exam, family obligations, out-of-town visitors—scheduled near the event date.
- You are a brand-new member of the organization.

If these or other special circumstances apply to you, don't volunteer this time. Someone else will do it. It's better to have no event at all than to manage (or attend) a poorly planned event. If you do take on the job but later realize you're not capable of running the event, talk with your chapter president immediately. Some solution can be worked out—don't just let the event fail.

Organization

"It's really all about organizing. If you have it all organized, generally nothing major will go wrong. If anything is left to chance, it will inevitably go wrong. You cannot trust the fates to work in your favor at all. They don't." So says Dr. Judy Green, vice president of communications and development for the Unitarian Universalist Association.

Veteran event managers agree: "Don't assume anything." Always ask and answer every possible question. Know in advance what, who, why, when, and how every detail of the event works, but allow for flexibility. Give as much attention to the creative as to the mechanical, as much to the human as to the physical demands of the project.

If the organization and advance preparations are well thought out and well executed, the entire event will be enjoyable. In fact, you will have gone a long way toward ensuring its success—and yours as a manager.

Advance Proposals
For many annual and international conventions, "bids" or "proposals" (written outlines of your plans for the event) are due years in advance. The American Camping Association starts planning a minimum of two years ahead for their national conference; the bidding takes place five years in advance.

Proposals are usually made to your national office (intensive efforts are sometimes made to secure votes from the membership as well). Your proposal should include fairly flexible descriptions of site, accommodations, program, and theme. (Again, the city or state convention board will be glad to assist, since bringing visitors into the area is their goal.)

Don't confirm any details until your proposal has been voted on, or you may end up paying cancellation fees. Use the proposal as the backbone of your event planning.

Your Event Record
Producing a successful event does involve paperwork. Don't be afraid of writing every detail down. Event managers all speak of the importance of lists. One event manager kept a huge sheet of paper as a master list at work (and a temporary list at home); whenever she thought of some new task, she would write it down. Not only did this clear her mind and keep her from worrying, she claims, but "you also get a real sense of accomplishment from crossing off an item once you've done it."

As soon as you begin to organize your event, you should begin your manager's report. (See Chapter 4, Evaluation and Report.) Use all of the blank forms provided in this book to put your event on paper. Work out your preliminary budget and put a copy of it in the file. (See Chapter 5, Financial Management.) When you choose the site, fill out a site survey form, photocopy it, and file it in a folder. (See Chapter 6, Site Selection.) Photocopy all your event paperwork and file it.

This accomplishes three things. You will get a very clear picture of how your event is shaping up if you review this folder regularly. You will only need to add post-mortem comments to this file in order to present it as your manager's report. And you will possess a copy of everything, just in case there are questions or problems.

Like many of her colleagues, Christine Simonsen, a professional event organizer in Pennsylvania, uses a large three-ring binder for each event. She creates a dozen or so divisions to organize her tasks and the associated paperwork:

- Timeline/Schedule
- Initial proposal
- Contacts
- Committees
- Correspondence
- Budget

- Site
- Marketing and promotion
- Promotional materials
- Registration
- Reception
- Theme and program (event specifics)
- Audiovisual

Carry your event binder with you at all times during the event. The binder should also contain your event schedule and program; menu; maps of the site and local area, showing stores, pay phones, and hospitals; and other vital information. Bring a copy of the insurance certificate of coverage to show just in case something goes wrong.

The Day of the Event

During the event, a manager should greet guests, visit at tables during the meal, discuss the sessions with seminar leaders, and generally see to it that everyone has the best possible time. Sharon Gallo, who runs the annual yard sale for the Trinity Baptist Church in Arlington, Massachusetts, keeps in constant motion during the day. "What I do is float—keep circling, collecting money. At each table, I ask: 'Is everything okay?' 'Do you need anything?' I try to keep my crew jovial."

Ideally, a manager will have delegated well enough to be able to do nothing but traverse the site, checking up on people and activities and chatting with guests to find out how the event is perceived. Establish a travel path that will cover the entire site at regular intervals. At outdoor sites and large events, event managers sometimes distribute walkie-talkies or wear beepers. Some physically challenged managers opt to remain at a central command post equipped with a telephone.

Problems "Every event you do, there's something unexpected. You just never know," warns Shelley Sommer.

Unforeseen disasters and emergencies at events happen all too often. At the first Baltimore City Fair in 1970, no one had remembered scissors for the ribbon-cutting ceremony, so state official Louis Goldstein borrowed a switchblade from a spectator.

Event managers have told me stories about problems with drunken guests, over-eager sprinkler systems, wrong desserts, and melting ice sculptures. Even more hair-raising tales: a transportation strike stranded more than 1,000 guests; half the guests didn't get the right room keys for several days; a hurricane, blizzard, or other weather problem canceled the event; a keynote speaker didn't show up at all; the event manager had emergency surgery—on the day of the event.

Keep a cool head (and back-up plans ready). All those event managers coped, and so will you. "The question at the time is not 'Why did this happen?' but 'How do we fix it?'" says Alicia Rodriguez. Time enough later, she adds, to determine the cause of the breakdown.

Remember what she said about needing "a good sense of humor"? Now you know why . . .

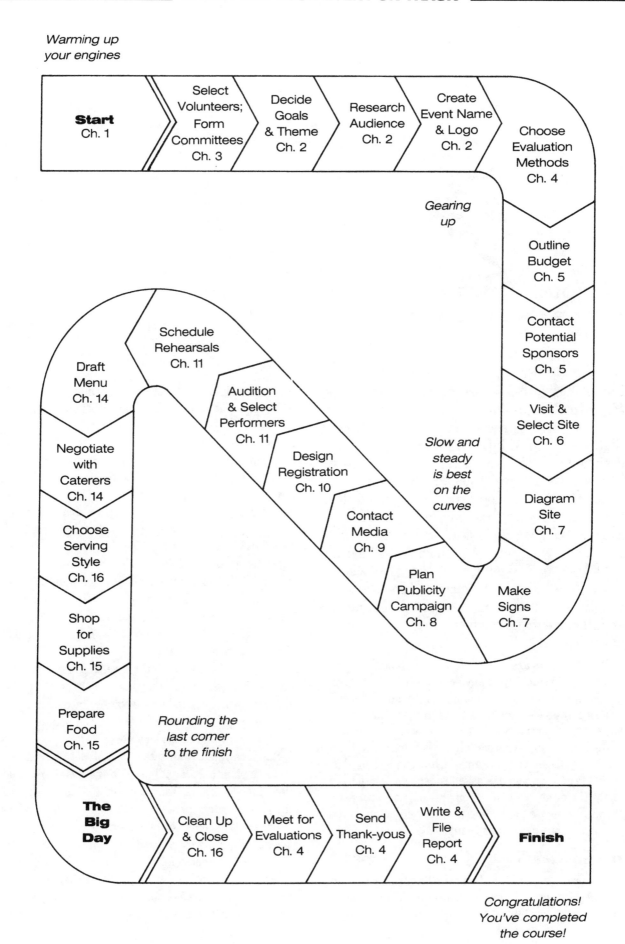

Warming up your engines

Start Ch. 1

Select Volunteers; Form Committees Ch. 3

Decide Goals & Theme Ch. 2

Research Audience Ch. 2

Create Event Name & Logo Ch. 2

Choose Evaluation Methods Ch. 4

Gearing up

Outline Budget Ch. 5

Contact Potential Sponsors Ch. 5

Visit & Select Site Ch. 6

Diagram Site Ch. 7

Slow and steady is best on the curves

Schedule Rehearsals Ch. 11

Draft Menu Ch. 14

Audition & Select Performers Ch. 11

Design Registration Ch. 10

Contact Media Ch. 9

Negotiate with Caterers Ch. 14

Choose Serving Style Ch. 16

Shop for Supplies Ch. 15

Plan Publicity Campaign Ch. 8

Make Signs Ch. 7

Prepare Food Ch. 15

Rounding the last corner to the finish

The Big Day

Clean Up & Close Ch. 16

Meet for Evaluations Ch. 4

Send Thank-yous Ch. 4

Write & File Report Ch. 4

Finish

Congratulations! You've completed the course!

Chapter

GOALS AND THEMES

Philip Harvey and James Snyder, writing in the *Harvard Business Review*, speak of the importance of goals: "A recent example in the United States is Farm Aid, the fundraising concerts designed to help distressed American farmers. The process was wonderful; hundreds of dedicated, well-intentioned people volunteered their time and talent for those in need. But practically no one focused on goals. Who was to be helped? In what manner? Would funds be used to bail out marginal farmers? Buy fertilizer? Make loans? These are tough and complicated questions that were only answered, if at all, as an afterthought to the more important process of raising funds."

Special events are labor-intensive and high-profile affairs. Unfortunately, many special events suffer from a lack of direction. Event managers can get so busy ordering supplies and enlisting volunteers that they forget the essential reason for the event.

Before you do any actual event planning, take time to think about why your organization is sponsoring this event. Whenever you are asked to make a decision about the event, return to your list of goals and your theme. Never plan anything that doesn't advance your goals or complement your theme.

Setting Goals

The organizers of the Seminole Tribal Fair in Florida keep two goals in mind. "The event is open to everyone—we want to educate people to our culture, to meet our neighbors, to show the community what we're all about. It's also a tribal event, a big reunion for our people," says Sandy Selner, secretary for the organizing committee.

Zeren Earls, director of First Night, an arts festival that attracts more than 100,000 people on New Year's Eve in Boston, Massachusetts, keeps her sights firmly set on the goals of her event: "Our mission statement is to deepen the appreciation of visual and performing arts. And I think we have done that; we're bringing the arts to a public forum . . . There is a unique concept here. It has an arts focus, it has a family focus, it has a nonalcoholic focus (there's no public drinking allowed). And we use public and historic places, indoors and outdoors to present the arts—city halls, churches, shop windows."

The *goal* of the event is the ultimate result you desire. The *goal measurements* recast the aims in clear, quantifiable, and time-related statements. The *strategies* are the detailed methods you use to reach your primary and secondary goals.

Suppose your organization, the Model Railroad Club, is planning an exhibition of the members' collection of model trains. Your primary *goal* is to educate the general public about model trains. You're also hoping to sign up some new members (a secondary goal). Your *goal measurements* would be in the form of statements such as: persuade at least 25 members to display their train sets at the event; sell 100 tickets to nonmembers in advance of the show. Your *strategies* would include: place two ads in the local newspaper; start a

---

Goals of Special Events & Conferences

■ Raise funds (for a specific cause, person, or place)

■ Build spirit among long-term members (heal a breach, solve a political problem, launch a new program)

■ Facilitate information distribution/exchange (especially for larger audiences)

■ Recruit new members (specific people or groups of people)

■ Celebrate (give awards, recognize volunteer efforts)

■ Attract publicity (reach new audiences, heighten public awareness)

---

sponsor program, so that each current member brings a prospective member to the event.

Especially in fundraising campaigns, make sure that your event is necessary and is the best way to accomplish what the organization needs and wants. Don't waste months of volunteer time to raise two dollars per member, if you could just ask the members for the money instead. Or, perhaps you could increase the admission or membership price for your film series, rather than organize a public festival.

Think seriously about why you want to produce this event. Take fundraising as an example: always know how much money you want to raise, what the money will be used for, who will benefit from the funds, and why your organization wants to raise funds through a special event rather than some other method.

Barbara Anderson, who volunteers for the Trinity Baptist Church in Arlington, Massachusetts, explains how the church participates in a local special event for the public: "We don't want to sell on Town Day. We could do a booth and make a lot of money. But we just want to promote that we're there for the community. So we dress up as clowns and give away balloons. We decided on that philosophy, hoping we'll be different and stand out in that respect. And we've gained some members that way."

Annual Events Sometimes, the goal of an annual event will change unnoticed. The Philadelphia Orchestra canceled its annual fundraising radio marathon after eight years because what began primarily as a fundraising event, with secondary public relations benefits, had become mostly a public relations exercise with little profit accrued. The reverse happens more frequently: an event created as a fellowship, recruitment, or public relations aid is a financial success. Each year the profit motive becomes more important,

until income from the event becomes a major part of the annual budget for the organization.

Audience ("Well, My Brother-in-Law Loves Scavenger Hunts")

You must balance the needs of the participants (who attend, buy tickets, and take part) with the needs of the sponsors (who contribute money, goods, or services). Research your audience, past events, and the goals of your organization to understand the wishes of your intended audience.

In Palm Beach, Florida, for example, organizers used a new twist on an old event to appeal to their wealthy audience. They held a black-tie car wash, complete with tuxedos and donated champagne, to benefit the American Foundation for AIDS Research.

Recruiting events are tailored specifically for non-members and should be fun and informational. The focus of any "open to the public" event must be the desires of the attendees, especially in cases where you charge an entrance fee. If you want to attract college students to your organization, for example, don't plan your event for a college vacation or exam period. Is your organization working for handicapped rights? Then don't hold your events at inaccessible halls. (Illinois and a few other states publish a list of handicapped-accessible sites and halls.)

Be sure to consider what people expect to experience at your event. A speech might be disappointing to the audience if they want to know about Scandinavian Christmas customs and your speaker tells them about your Scandinavian church's work with Salvadoran refugees. Some people who request presentations *do* want to learn about the club and how it works. Other clients may have different expectations. School performances, for example, should be carefully geared to the age of your listeners. Research the audience with your client before you plan the event.

Children Certain events, such as fairs and bazaars, welcome children. If children are expected, include activities aimed at their age group. Serious banquets and conferences are generally not for children. A no-children-allowed policy must be stated in the publicity for these events. When appropriate, be firm about unattended minors at your event and insist that they be accompanied by a parent or guardian.

Financial Sponsors Before you enlist financial sponsors, find out what they expect in return for their support. Do they want their business logo prominently displayed? Do they assume that their vice president will be the featured banquet speaker? Reach a consensus and make sure you get your plans approved by the relevant parties involved.

Types of Events

When managers are volunteers, they enjoy flexibility concerning the kind of event they want to create. But perhaps your minister doesn't approve of raffles, or your volunteers can't cook—these factors will shape your theme and programming.

There are many ways to categorize event types: local or regional, traditional or original, indoor or outdoor. Many areas sustain traditional events, held at the same time each year. A parade and fireworks on the Fourth of July are important annual rituals in many small towns. Certain customs attach to long-lived events. They are good events for neophyte managers to take on because they are relatively easy to run. (To invigorate a timeworn event, change the site, menu, or entertainment—but not all at once.) When you accrue more experience as a manager, you may move on to larger, more original events.

Selecting an Event Your choice of a specific event will rest on three supports: your purpose (fundraising, recruitment, etc.); your audience (needs and characteristics); and your organization (success lies in using your strongest resources).

For example, appropriate special events for historical societies include trivia games based on local history; tours of historical homes; re-creations and plays of historic incidents; classes in antique restoration; and period, costumed fairs. Many libraries hold children's events, featuring a reading workshop and prizes for best costume character from a book. This is a subtle way to encourage literary interest. Such events are clearly connected to the mission of the organization and can draw on the talents and knowledge of members. Events that depend on outside agencies and unfamiliar audiences are usually more difficult and less successful.

Special events held by organizations and clubs can center on such elements as:

- Food (bake sales, potlucks, award banquets, cooking seminars)
- Entertainment (talent shows, concerts, theater parties, gospel sings, film series, pageants)
- Merchandise (rummage sales, flea markets, yard sales, auctions, vendor booths)
- Athletic endeavors (tennis tournaments, marathons, team sports, races)
- Education (seminars, conferences, lectures, workshops, lessons, meetings)
- Games (bridge, backgammon, beano, raffles, board games, chess, bingo)
- Potpourri (picnics, fairs, bazaars, field days)

As you can see, the possibilities are endless.

Choosing a Theme

Develop a theme for your event. Hobbies and careers, holidays, seasons, games, activities, history, costumes, ethnic cultures, geography, colors, flowers, jewels, literature, weddings, saints' days, and theology can all form the bases for special events. Books such as *Chase's Annual Events* can provide you with plenty of ideas. (See Resources.)

A Valentine's Day Dance where everyone is asked to wear the color red or a "Holly Christmas" church bazaar are simple theme events. Or, your Model Railroad Club may decide the theme for its show will be "Travel Through Time." Some events emphasize a time period, with names like "Class Reunion and '50s Sock Hop" and "Annual Founders' Day Picnic."

Date The date itself may suggest a theme. In April alone, the calendar lists April Fool's Day, International Children's Book Day, Bike Safety Week, Arbor Day, St. George's Feast Day, National Coin Week, National Guitar Week, World Health Day, and National Library Week. In Indianapolis, the Muscular Dystrophy Association persuaded Internal Revenue Service officials to be dunk tank targets at an event held just before the April tax filing deadline. The season can provide inspiration, too. In September, major events in Illinois echo the fall weather: Wolf Road Prairie Festival, Pioneer Autumn, Annual Nauvoo Grape Festival, and Union County Sportsman's Weekend.

Site The site of an event may contribute to theme ideas, as it did for the National Society of Fund Raising Executives. The 1989 NSFRE International Conference of Fund Raising was held at the Disneyland Hotel in Anaheim, California. The conference theme was "It's a Small, Small World"—the title of one of the park rides and the feeling NSFRE hoped to inspire in their participants.

Names and Logos Choose the name of your event with great care. Avoid clichés. Use a memorable name that clearly explains and identifies your event, and be sure not to infringe on another organization's copyright or registered trademark. Your "Town Day" will not stand out among 15 other events with the same name, but "Centerville's Mardi Gras" might capture some attention. Here are some examples of good event names:

- "San Francisco Hill Stride" (California)
- "Great American Chocolate Festival" (Pennsylvania)
- "Jambalaya Jamboree" (Louisiana)
- "Reenactment Chickamauga Battlefield" (Tennessee)
- "Lights, Camera, Auction" (Ohio)
- "Carowinds Clogging Championship" (North Carolina)
- "Common Ground Fair" (Maine)
- "Corn Palace Stampede Rodeo" (South Dakota)

Many event organizers dwell on the importance of theme and of coordinating all print materials, from invitations through programs, tickets, signs, table settings, and correspondence. A "logo" or "graphic identity" (visual identification or representation) for your event will aid your advertising efforts with audience recognition. Even the smallest event can put a logo to good use. Logos should be simple, imaginative, and memorable, and must reproduce well both in color and black and white.

Develop your logo from the theme and purpose of the event. Your logo for "Travel Through Time" could be a train running on the "outside track" of a clockface, using old-fashioned type. Project Bread's 19th Annual Walk for Hunger logo featured a heart resting in a running shoe; the theme was "Heart and Sole." If you are unable to come up with a good design, use the organization logo and the event name. (See Illustration 3, Event Logos, in this chapter.)

Atmosphere One of the manager's tasks is to maintain the atmosphere of an event. This means more than just seeing to the physical surroundings and the preparation of the food; it includes the "feel" of the event as well. Arranging the musical selections is just as important as counting the electrical appliances at the site. Every detail, no matter how minute, contributes to the appropriate atmosphere—or lack thereof.

Marion Denby was a volunteer event manager for more than twenty years before she started a very suc-cessful business, The Planned Event, in Washington, D.C. "Theme is a very tricky situation," according to Denby. "How can you make it exciting? There's a lot you can do, but you always have to worry about the budget. Work around your restrictions. And always coordinate everything."

Music, costumes, decorations, and programming pull together in color and style to enhance and empha-size the theme. Choose one or two colors for the event, one dominant color and one accent, plus white or black. Use true contrasts or two different shades of one hue.

Keep decorations simple and tasteful. In large halls with lots of people, only large decorations—preferably at head height or higher—show up. Balloons, crepe paper, and large-scale photos can provide maximum impact and color on a small budget. Flags, bunting, travel or theme posters, slides, and other graphics can be strategically placed to transform your site.

In *Reprise: The Extraordinary Revival of Early Music*, authors Joel Cohen and Herb Snitzer discuss "Renaissance Fayres": "The most successful such undertaking in my experience took place in a medieval walled village of Southern France a few years ago . . . Just as important as the costumes and the music in creating an illusion of earlier times was the temporary but total absence of automobiles. In America, it is harder to do a Renaissance Fayre, but that doesn't stop us from trying."

Lighting Clever lighting can help spotlight a per-former or speaker, encourage intimate conversation, or display artwork to advantage. Tiny white Christmas lights, sometimes called "fairy lights," can be used to outline architecture or twinkle in foliage. Removing bulbs from certain fixtures while adding colored bulbs or light-colored theater gels helps convey your theme. Candlelight is always more flattering and will lend an old-fashioned glow. Dimming the lighting in the hall, or turning lights off completely, is a proven way to quiet noise or focus attention.

Props Borrow costumes and props from amateur theater groups. Learn from profit-making businesses: for a "Fête de France" promotion, Bloomingdale's bor-rowed ethnic costumes from a museum.

Favors "Table favors" can be edible (see Chapter 14, Planning a Meal), floral, practical, or decorative. Your "Travel Through Time" event could use small plastic boxcars to hold after-dinner mints or display flowers. Number favors unobtrusively, then pick

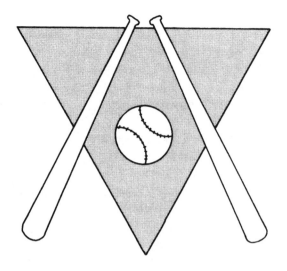

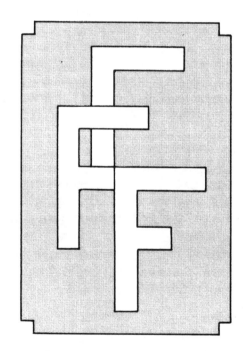

random numbers to determine door prizes. Auction off particularly attractive centerpieces, or give them away to your hardest workers at the end of the event.

Date and Time

Listen to Christine Simonsen, volunteer for the Society of Arts and Crafts, deciding a date for "Threads: An Exhibition of Wearable Art": "We wanted it to be one of the first events of the fall season—a kickoff fall fundraising event. To choose a specific date, we looked at the social calendar and we checked with all the other arts organizations. Of course, we took into consideration the availability of the hotel and our celebrity emcee. In June, we mailed a 'save-the-date' card (asking them to hold the date on their calendars, with information to come). We mailed the invitations to arrive right after the Labor Day weekend, so that we got in on the ground floor with people getting back from the summer holidays."

You will need at least two months' preparation time, even for very small events. Preparations for the next annual event should begin as the report for the last annual event is submitted. Lead time can be telescoped for rush jobs or emergencies, but even hard work can't always make up the difference.

Use common sense as you set the date for your event. You can check the local weather bureau for predictions of wet and dry dates. Avoid scheduling events on holiday weekends when many of your would-be guests are traveling out of town (unless a holiday attracts people to your area). A local Unitarian Universalist Church took advantage of a Michigan State University policy; dorms do not serve food on Sunday evenings, so the church began a "MSU Sunday Supper Series."

The best time to hold a recruitment meeting is about a month before a local event or meeting, so that interested people can attend a full-scale organization event shortly after the new member presentation.

Competition Try not to schedule similar events in competition with other organizations. Charlotte, North Carolina, boasts several horse shows in three summer months, all free and at the same site, but note how they differ in sponsor and audience:

- Open Show (Boy Scout Troop 42)
- Charity "A" Rated Hunter Show (Knights of Columbus)
- Paso Fino Show (Piedmont Paso Fino Association)

- Exhibitors Association Show (N.C. Palomino Association)
- "C" Rated Hunter-Jumper Show (Mecklenburg Hounds)

Check listings in last year's newspapers to avoid conflicting with other organizations' annual events. The Pittsburgh Cultural Trust operates a calendar of events clearinghouse for that region of Pennsylvania. The *Houston Black Book* keeps track of many categories of events, including corporate and special retail promotions in Texas. The *California Calendar* lists events in California. And the National Event Clearinghouse maintains a nationwide database of thousands of events (see Resources).

Organizations that are funded by the United Way must refrain from certain fundraising events during the local campaign period. "The United Way has guidelines which restrict or which cover fundraising activities for their funded charities. If you're a United Way funded agency, you want to be sure to consult with your local United Way to see what their guidelines are—they vary from United Way to United Way," indicates Bette Rossen, a United Way manager in Massachusetts.

Holidays Unless your event theme or purpose fits in with these holidays, don't use these dates.

Miss or Match Days

- Mother's or Father's Day (Sunday, May and June)
- Good Friday (Friday, March or April)
- Easter (Sunday, March or April)
- Passover (March or April)
- Memorial Day (last Monday in May)
- High school/college graduation days (May and June)
- Fourth of July (entire weekend)
- Labor Day (first weekend in September)
- Rosh Hashanah (mid-September or early October)
- Yom Kippur (ten days after Rosh Hashanah)
- Thanksgiving Day (fourth Thursday in November)
- Chanukah (December)
- Christmas Day, and up to two weeks beforehand

These are generally "at-home" family days with visiting relatives. However, when these holidays fall on a weekend, the day before or after is often an attractive option. The Black Hills Balloon Rally in South Dakota is held on Mother's Day weekend and is quite popular.

Day and Time Consider what day of the week—and what time of day—is best for your audience. Are you trying to reach professional women? Hold your open house immediately after work. How many hours can you expect children to sit quietly? If you're looking for a family day, try Saturday or Sunday afternoons. If you're not selling lunches, don't start before noon. If you're not planning dinner, don't expect guests to stay after about 5 P.M.

Chapter **3**
VOLUNTEERS AND STAFF

"The committee is all in it together, but the chair must know *the buck stops here*. A volunteer chairperson has a lot of authority," counsels Marion Denby, long-time event manager. Sharon Gallo, church volunteer, supports this view: "You need one person to step in and decide problems, maintain control. Everybody should know who's in charge."

On the day of the event, for example, the event manager must not leave the site until the event is over. Rule Number One: *You* are the manager. You can always find volunteers to do last-minute shopping or other off-site chores. You need to be present to deal with any emergency.

Because it is impossible for you to do everything yourself, you are responsible for choosing people to help you. An event manager's ability to recruit loyal, thrifty, brave, and competent persons to supervise individual areas is crucial. Be discriminating. Find capable assistants whose reliability will allow you to manage "the big picture."

"It's really easy to get people to volunteer for a one-time event versus having them do, say, a newsletter—even though it might take the same amount of time. You have to look at it through their eyes. People want to do something, then be done with it," is the view of one discerning event organizer.

Assess skills, and then fit the person to the task. For example, the most organized and capable person is inadequate as a kitchen manager unless she or he knows the difference between onions and potatoes, so select a kitchen manager who has a solid working knowledge of cooking and kitchen operations. On the other hand, don't waste talented cooks as ticket salespeople, unless they want to try something new and different. Some skills are transferable (for example, artistic sense is an advantage on decorating crews or publicity crews).

The Administrative Committee

Most groups use a branching committee structure, with the event manager as chairperson of the administrative committee. (For large events, you may add a co-chairperson.) Other members of the administrative committee are assigned to specific areas of responsibility; they then assemble their own crews. The chair position on the administrative committee may be rotated each year among the members of the committee.

Craig Macfarlane, president of the Boston Road Club, believes, "You really need to create a relationship with the person before you can ask him or her to do something." Friends are your first natural resource for committee members, but don't stack the deck. When recruiting your administrative committee, look for volunteers with leadership ability, since they'll be responsible for persuading, supervising, and managing a crew. Try to balance personalities, too. Although commitment is important, a whole room full of over-enthusiastic types can become quite wearing.

Many high-ticket benefit committees insist on "deep-pocket" financial status as a criterion for participation, and thus risk ignoring useful workers. Remember, *everyone* contributes in a volunteer organization.

Community-wide events usually draft business people (because of their resources) and representatives (members of the intended audience). For the "Canine Walk," a fundraising event for the Muscular Dystrophy Association in Massachusetts, the organizing committee was carefully selected, according to regional coordinator Catherine Kokoski. "What made it work was that from the start we developed a committee that included the dog officers, a veterinarian, and someone from the Society for the Prevention of Cruelty to Animals—all the groups that, if we didn't include them, might have gotten complaints about animal cruelty."

Be honest in advance about the demands of the job. The schedules in the front of each relevant chapter outline the particular responsibilities. Give each prospective member of the administrative committee a job description and schedule when you interview them. Discuss any time constraints: will committee members be able to attend the monthly evening meetings? Are they relatively free during the crucial periods?

Negotiate how much creativity and leeway you will grant. For example, kitchen managers come in different flavors with different titles (see Chapter 14, Planning a Meal): food and beverage chairperson, hospitality officer, refreshments committee. Some act as co-managers and are in on all the planning from the beginning. They shoulder with you the responsibility for planning the menu and the budget, and also do the shopping and run the kitchen. Another brand of manager is simply given the menu and the supplies with which to produce the food on the day of the event; his or her function is to supervise the cooks and crew, seeing that the food is properly prepared. If you are hiring a caterer or using the on-site banquet manager, your kitchen manager's responsibilities will change accordingly. But, whatever type you choose, make your expectations clear beforehand.

Division of Responsibilities

Structure your volunteer teams in whatever way makes the most sense for the event. (See Illustration 4, Committee Organization, in this chapter for a typical design.) One church is trying out a unique system for their Sunday lunches. They form three teams: for one event, Team 1 chooses the menu, shops, cooks, and serves; Team 2 takes over cleanup; Team 3 sits out. On a rotation scheme like this, a team enjoys a well-

deserved rest every third event. A team leader observes, "We're trying to divide the teams more evenly. Some core people who know what they're doing should be on each team; we also divide people into groups that are more friendly with each other and work better together. Now each team tries to outdo the others when it's their turn."

Every job you delegate means one you won't need to do yourself, and one more person who has a small stake in the success of the event. The Baltimore City Fair, for example, keeps some 2,000 volunteers busy.

Kimberly Kayser oversees events for the American Cancer Society in Massachusetts. She explains why pledge events are labor-intensive: "You need a lot of volunteers to do the clerical aspect. All these people who say yes, they're going to donate, have to be billed. It's a tremendous process—you can send out thousands of bills—and then it has to be followed up. I think a lot of times people don't realize that."

Recruit enough people beforehand to fill the majority of the jobs. Get firm commitments from them. Don't rely on last-minute volunteers to fill important jobs. Back-up volunteers and understudies are good for on-the-spot small tasks, such as mixing bowls of punch or taking a garbage can around the hall every so often. It's a good idea to leave a sign-up sheet at the registration table with specific job areas, such as ushering and cleanup, listed for last-minute helpers.

Never turn down offers of help. Mobilize spouses, children, and other organizations for your public event. The Rangeley Wild Mountain Time Festival in Maine coordinates several groups, including the Masons (breakfast), the Firemen's Auxiliary (lunch), and the Rangeley Friends of the Performing Arts (concert and a contest). In Michigan, 45 community theater groups from all over the state contribute about 1,000 volunteers to the International Festival of Theatre.

A word of caution: negotiate joint responsibilities in detail, including use of names in publicity, use of membership lists, number of volunteers promised, profit and loss shares. Write a letter of agreement, and get it signed by the officials of all organizations involved.

Meetings A twelve-person committee directs the annual Seminole Tribal Fair in Florida, which pulls in 20,000 people. The committee meets every few weeks during the year and once a week as the date approaches—a common schedule for many special events committees. Send informative agendas in advance, and you'll find many problems solved and questions answered before the meeting.

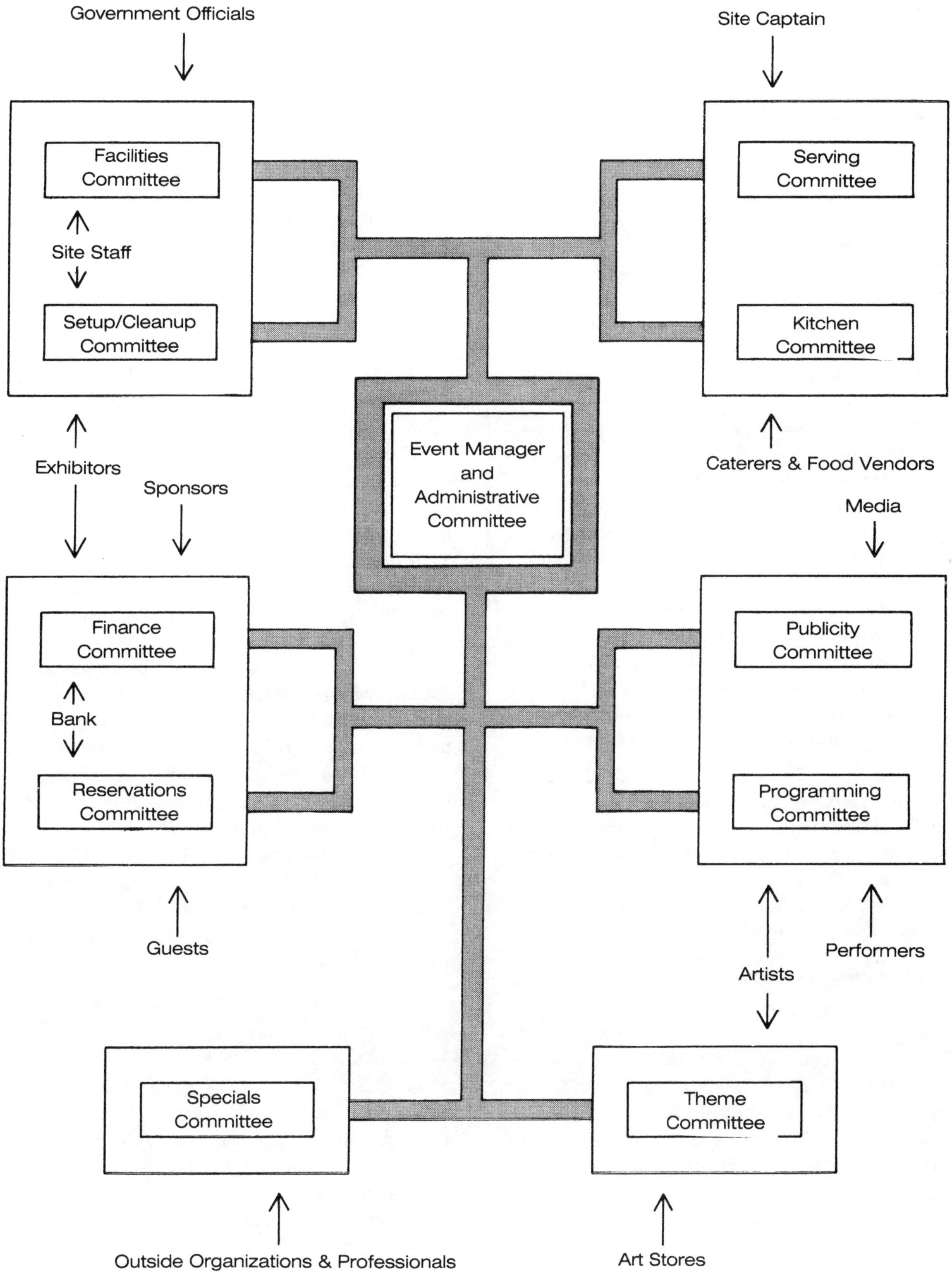

Government Officials

Site Captain

Facilities
Committee

↑
Site Staff
↓

Setup/Cleanup
Committee

Serving
Committee

Kitchen
Committee

Event Manager
and
Administrative
Committee

Exhibitors

Sponsors

Caterers & Food Vendors

Media

Finance
Committee

↑
Bank
↓

Reservations
Committee

Publicity
Committee

Programming
Committee

Guests

Artists

Performers

Specials
Committee

Theme
Committee

Outside Organizations & Professionals

Art Stores

Standard Committees

- Administrative Committee: coordinates everything, evaluates event, writes final report.
- Theme and Decorations: develops theme, decorates site.
- Finance/Business: receives and deposits checks, pays bills, solicits sponsors and exhibitors, keeps books.
- Facilities/Security/Parking: selects and reserves site, diagrams facilities, contacts government officials, obtains permits.
- Publicity/Media Relations: writes press releases and newsletter announcements, creates posters and handbills, designs display windows and advertisements, handles media relations.
- Reservations/Hosts/Reception: sells tickets, tracks reservations, greets guests.
- Kitchen/Refreshments: plans menu, shops, cooks.
- Serving: assigns servers, borrows and returns inventory supplies, serves food.
- Programming/Directing: selects and schedules programming, rehearses performers, presides over ceremonies, designs and produces printed programs.
- Setup/Cleanup: assigns exhibit space, hires custodial staff, moves furniture, cleans and closes site.
- Specials: costume designer, prompter, and props keeper for plays; a veterinarian for animal shows; spotters and runners for auctions; ward officers, ballot distributors, and credential checkers for caucuses.

Please start your meetings on time! Discuss important items, not trivia, and define clearly who should be doing what and when. Check on any over-enlistment of crew members, prime enthusiasm, revise scheduling as needed, and redistribute the workload if it becomes too much for any one individual.

Motivating Volunteers

One development officer uses the term "friendraising" to explain her event management strategy. Volunteers have actually met while working on events and subsequently married. A volunteer admits, "The only reason why I do that particular event (which I hate) is because the organizer is a good friend. We help each other in our different projects—or else you wouldn't see me there."

For one phone-a-thon, telephone solicitors were teamed up by profession (e.g., lawyers versus schoolteachers). The volunteers felt more comfortable,

according to the organizer, and it created a competitive edge so more money was raised. Many fundraising experts advocate forms of rivalry (posting lists, awarding prizes) to encourage volunteers to sell tickets or program advertisements. There's nothing wrong with quotas tied to deadlines—that's good planning, so you can redistribute ad pages or tickets in time to sell effectively. But your methods should not extend to public humiliation, such as marking out the "laziest" volunteer salesperson with a button or token.

The key words in a manager's vocabulary are *persuade* and *cajole*, not *demand* or *expect*. Never command. Always request. Joan Volunteer might have been counting on your very event as the one where she could relax and enjoy herself for once. No matter how enthusiastic the reply to your request, always recheck before the event in time to make other plans if something or someone has fallen through.

As much as possible, rotate your work force; don't expect volunteers to work during the entire event, no matter how dedicated. Give volunteers a chance to enjoy the event as well as sample the drudgery.

People are more willing to help if they know that they will only be involved in one or two aspects of the work. Dolly Ladd works in the development office of Saint Andrew's School in Bethesda, Maryland. She finds her pool of volunteers (mothers of students) shrinking rapidly. "More and more women are going back to work, so they have less and less time available to help." Her solution? "I designed volunteer responsibilities so that everything is a short-term job. I don't want to waste my people's time."

Remember that your helpers have lives outside the organization, too. Don't expect your volunteers to be absent from paid employment because of the event or to spend every free moment on the event. And that goes for you, too.

Attitude Foster a team attitude. Provide light refreshments during planning meetings, and always leave time after business for socializing. Memorize every volunteer's name. (How would you like to be working hard and have your boss say "Hey, you"?) Delegate small problems as they arise. Handle large ones decisively and immediately. Communicate plans to your administrative committee, and urge them to distribute any information and printed materials to their crews. Many managers seem to expect helpers to "read minds." Each worker must understand *why* each task is necessary, *how* it should be done, and *when* it fits into the schedule.

Appearance Set an example for your volunteers and staff. Dress comfortably but neatly on the day of your event. If you're the kitchen manager, wear an apron in the kitchen and put on your clean jacket before appearing in the public areas of the site. Event managers should wear a bright color to stand out from the crowd. "I wear sneakers until the last possible moment," confesses one event manager.

At formal events, stick with white shirts and dark pants or skirts for servers. Some event managers use colored name tags or buttons to distinguish event organizers. For less formal events, you can give event workers free T-shirts, aprons, hats, or armbands in the theme colors of the event. Omni Hotels issues a small golden gavel pin to meeting managers.

Paid Staff and Outside Agencies

By all means, consider using volunteers from programs such as the Retired Senior Volunteer Program, but don't waste their time or experience. Ask them to help with a *specific* problem or project. If you imagine that you are actually paying them by the hour, you'll learn the right attitude.

Performers, speakers, caterers, and specialized staff may all be required for your event. Ask the relevant national trade association to recommend local professionals (see Resources). Many organizations choose to hire a part-time clerk or secretary to deal with the paperwork of the event.

Use a simple letter of agreement with all paid staff and outside agencies to prevent misunderstandings. Include the following information:

■ Date, name, and place of event
■ Type and length of performance, service, product
■ Fees, expenses, deposits
■ Cancellations and refund policy
■ Starting and ending times
■ Refreshment and break arrangements

Chapter President or Coordinator The chapter president or a paid staff member is usually the legal representative of the organization in your area and the best source of information concerning procedures and traditions. So, meet regularly or submit frequent progress reports. Within a few weeks after the event, your final report should be submitted to the chapter president and/or other relevant organization officers.

Outside Agencies Laws and regulations must be obeyed if the organization is to exist peacefully in the real world. As a manager, you will want to be familiar with the organization's liability insurance policy. Inform the local police about your event and discuss parking and traffic policies. Some municipalities will expect a registration fee if you serve alcohol or other refreshments at your event. Permits and licenses may be demanded by various branches of the government.

Volunteers Versus Staff The biggest problems between volunteers and staff stem from confusion over roles, which leads to unrealistic expectations on both sides. The turnover rate for both categories of workers doesn't help, either. Staff may well hold different priorities; respect their deadlines and teach them to respect yours. If necessary, meet regularly with staff to outline division of tasks.

Vendors "In terms of caterers or most vendors, I either go by reputation or by price," says Hannah Roberts, a former director of alumni relations whose most recent accomplishment was the Newport Vintage Dance Holiday in Rhode Island. "If you want to buy a lot of balloons, you figure a balloon is a balloon, so you're just out for the best deal. Look through the Yellow Pages, and make a list of who sells balloons. There are extra conveniences—Do they deliver the helium tank? Do they charge extra for the little nozzle to blow up the balloons? Are they going to give you the colors you want or do they only stock ugly colors? Sometimes, as with balloons, I'm not so concerned about references. But when choosing a caterer, I usually won't choose one without a reference."

Trainees (Teach Someone Else— You Deserve a Vacation)

To develop skilled event managers, many groups endorse some kind of manager-in-training program. At Hawaii's Punahou School, the annual Carnival is a project of the junior class. Parents of juniors assume booth and division chairs; parents of sophomores serve as co-chairs in training for next year.

Advancement to more responsible positions is often used as a reward for dedicated workers. Novices who volunteer as ushers for First Night Boston may be "promoted" to house managers after their first year.

Or, volunteers graduate from running small, casual meetings or events to producing larger events, and finally to overseeing full-blown national conferences, high-ticket fundraisers, or annual celebrations. The simple event will give you practice in planning the more complicated one.

Sometimes, novice managers are assigned to work with experienced managers for an event prior to their own. For example, each member of the administrative committee may enlist an understudy. The experienced manager does not necessarily share responsibilities with the trainee, but the trainee audits all the major preparations. This provides valuable experience to new managers.

Other groups assign experienced managers as "advisors" or "mentors" to all new managers. Even if there is no formal deputy program in your organization, consider asking a manager-in-training to work with you for your event. Good managers are always in short supply, but they are a renewable resource.

And get as much training as you can for yourself, too. Urge your organization to pay for courses and subscriptions (see Resources). The more you know, the more your organization will benefit—and the more you can teach other volunteers and staff.

Chapter **4**
EVALUATION AND REPORT

Christine Simonsen, volunteer event manager for the Society of Arts and Crafts, counts her blessings after a fashion show and dessert dance: "No crises, no emergencies, no one fell off the runway, all the band members showed up, no food poisoning, no accidents to or from the event . . . "

Evaluation is a step that is often ignored or misunderstood when applied to nonprofit special events. As one event manager prefaced his remarks about evaluation, "Well, the most immediate way to evaluate is to count the number of people who show up." Of course, the attendance and profit figures provide a definite indication of success or failure, but other measures can be equally important. Many fundraising events are judged solely on profit, disregarding other factors, such as the level of personal satisfaction of the invited public. Or, sadly, many new member events are judged on how many names and addresses are gathered, not on how many viable members actually join and contribute to the organization.

Critiquing the Event

Plan your evaluation at the beginning of your event. Decide which statistics you care about, and make sure your staff keeps accurate records. The primary goal of your event is the main factor to evaluate. If you want to review your media effectiveness, place a guest book at the registration table so attendees can record where or how they heard about the event. Or, as Claudia

Laverty, regional recruitment specialist for the Red Cross, points out, "Scheduling is a really important factor in the success of blood drives. We try and get it evenly scheduled throughout, so there's a good donor flow and things don't get backed up. We always talk about scheduling." The evaluation form for blood drives, therefore, includes the question: "Were donors scheduled for specific times?"

To evaluate your event, you must return to your original brainstorming and event planning. What were your goals? Have they been reached? What new strategies did you use? Did they work? You will need some feedback from all parties involved: paid staff, volunteers, participants, performers or speakers, exhibitors and vendors, the local community, financial sponsors, the site owners and workers. It is always important to know if your volunteers felt appreciated, if your staff felt overworked, if your audience perceived the event as it was planned. For this purpose, you use surveys, questionnaires, and interviews.

Fast evaluation by key staff and volunteers is important to Catherine Kokoski, regional coordinator for the Muscular Dystrophy Association, "so that it's still fresh in everyone's mind."

Administrative Committee Hold a meeting of the administrative committee within a few weeks after the event takes place. Do some factual investigating. Was attendance higher or lower than expected? (And do you know why?) What were food costs? Did the photographs reproduce well? How many people attended

---

Common Evaluation Questions

- Did attendees enjoy the event?
- Were they made to feel welcome?
- Was participation active and thoughtful?
- How did they feel about the organization before the event? After the event?
- Who was the best speaker?
- What was the best seminar?
- Did they like the location?
- How was the food?
- What was the most important part of the event?
- What part of the event was unnecessary?
- Did they think they "got their money's worth"?
- Would they attend the event again?
- Was the event at a good time of year, month, week, day?
- Would they recommend this event to other people?
- Any suggestions for improving the event?

---

each session or lecture or film? What supplies, if any, were completely used up? What couldn't you *give* away? How fast was the registration process? (And could it be improved?)

Participants Informal, random interviewing *during* the event is often recommended, because people will give you on-the-spot impressions. But Stephen Erickson, who works on conferences for both the National Council of University Research Administrators and the Research Administration Discussion Group, disagrees: "I don't believe in instant evaluation. Because you're going to get people who really hated the speaker—or for whatever reason, they're going to give it a really negative evaluation. Or, they could give it a glowing evaluation without having given the session a whole lot of real thought or reflection."

He's right in one respect: you can't rely solely on instant evaluation because by its nature it is flawed. However, by asking questions during the event, you can pick up valuable clues for later, more in-depth probing. Also, you can find mistakes that can be corrected immediately so that the event runs more smoothly.

"Focus groups" (groups of eight to ten attendees led by a knowledgeable moderator, informally discussing the event) and questionnaires can be used to gather more lasting feelings and information after the event.

For example, an evaluation form for a convention of people interested in historic dance included questions on each class and teacher, each band, social events, housing accommodations, and meals. Some groups

send different evaluations to different audiences; vendors and presenters, for example, usually possess disparate concerns and opinions.

"We put the evaluation form right in the participant's registration packet," states Terry Phinney, regional executive director for the American Camping Association. She plans yearly regional conferences and is gearing up for hosting the national conference. "We've done it two ways: usually, a general evaluation, rating facilities, food, flow, program; and occasionally we do a more specific evaluation on each session. During the course of the conference, we keep saying, 'Don't forget your evaluation forms!' We put a box near the exit. Very often, two or three weeks later, we'll get a few more in the mail . . . I think they are vitally important."

Stephen Erickson adds, "The purpose of the evaluation is not only to see how you've done—most people can tell—but how you can improve for the future." Make sure you actually *do* incorporate suggestions into future events, or you will frustrate your respondents—after wasting their time and your own.

Official Reports

A manager's report reflects the organization of the entire event. Basically, you'll photocopy the contents of your event binder and add any comments that you feel will be helpful. This report should be submitted to the chapter president within two months of your event. Some groups require that you send a complete financial report to the national treasurer within thirty days of the event.

Write as thorough but concise a report as possible; these reports are a valuable resource for future managers. Just as you researched past event reports in order to plan your event properly, so other managers will utilize your report to predict attendance, estimate budget figures, and schedule activities. It's common practice for organizations to keep manager's reports as part of the official files. A well-done manager's report from you will help ensure good events for your group in the future.

Permanent Records Keep some visual record of every special event you run, both for your own information and to use as public relations and publicity material for the organization. At least one photographer should work your event. More elaborate events need more elaborate methods of recording.

```
┌─ Event Report Structure ──────────────┐
│ ■ Summary sheet (paragraph synopsis from each │
│   committee)                           │
│ ■ Committee and crew lists, sponsor list │
│ ■ Budget worksheets (with all receipts attached) │
│ ■ Site survey, with attached diagrams, map, and │
│   directions                           │
│ ■ Copies of all printed matter and publicity │
│ ■ Schedule (annotated to indicate what worked and │
│   what didn't)                         │
│ ■ Program (and biographies of performers and │
│   presenters)                          │
│ ■ Vendor sheet (business cards and rate sheets for │
│   each)                                │
│ ■ Menu and recipes (quantities, leftovers, and prices │
│   are especially pertinent) or caterer's information │
│ ■ Suggestions and miscellaneous (you will probably │
│   discover something new and/or more efficient at │
│   your event, so pass it along)        │
└───────────────────────────────────────┘
```

If you decide to film or videotape a meeting or special event, make all arrangements in advance with the audiovisual crew. Agree beforehand on required equipment and priority of tasks. (For example, you *must* make videotapes of the president greeting the seminar leaders, you're less interested in the seminar presentations, and you don't want any taping done during the banquet.) If you're concerned about guests tripping on cables or being bothered by hot lights, confer with the crew. Professionals may be able to use battery-powered video cameras or special cameras that will work under available lighting.

Expressing Appreciation

Zeren Earls knows how hard her volunteers work at First Night in Boston, an annual event that begins in the early afternoon December 31st and ends at midnight. "We thank the volunteers. We give a party which runs from 11 P.M. to 2 A.M. As they finish their work, they have a place to come to wind down and eat."

Prompt, personal, handwritten or telephoned thank-yous for all your volunteers and contributors are a must. A general written thank-you in the membership newsletter or local newspaper is a nice touch; everyone worked to make your event special. Your grateful letter to ad program sponsors should include a "tear sheet" (a copy of the ad as it appeared in the program).

Personal Evaluation (Who Won—You or the Event?)

There, you've done it! You're an event manager. Not only should you evaluate the event, you should also evaluate yourself. Ask yourself the following questions:

■ Was I a good boss?
■ Was it worth it?
■ Did I keep complete notes and fill out all the paperwork?
■ Did I miss any deadlines?
■ Was the event a success or failure?
■ What parts of the job did I like best?
■ What parts did I dislike?
■ Which people did I work with well?
■ Which people will I never work with again?
■ Do I want to manage another event?

It is not wise to begin immediately on another event. But if you intend to manage the same event again, you should jot down some ideas and prohibitions for next time while the event is fresh in your mind. One such manager's notes read: "Think about better name tags." "Number of microphones should equal number of panelists." "Change schedule." "Tell hotel re mikes, changes in schedule, vegetarian lunches were never made up."

Whether or not the event was a success, you undoubtedly learned a lot. And there's *always* room for improvement.

5. FINANCIAL MANAGER'S SCHEDULE

Timing	Task
5-12 months prior to event	■ Open official bank account. ■ Pay site deposit and other advance fees.
3-5 months prior	■ Figure preliminary budget with chairperson. ■ Meet monthly with committee. ■ Determine fee schedules with registrar. ■ Mail invoices to exhibitors and vendors.
2-3 months prior	■ Meet monthly with committee. ■ Pay for permits, licenses, etc. ■ Pay bills, deposit fees.
1-2 months prior	■ Meet monthly with committee. ■ Finalize budget. ■ List donors and sponsors for program. ■ Pay bills, deposit fees.
1 month prior	■ Meet with committee. ■ Confirm all arrangements and contracts. ■ Pay bills, deposit fees.
1 week prior	■ Meet with committee. ■ Deposit last of advance reservation fees. ■ Get final count from registration manager.
EVENT DAY	■ Pick up small bills and change from bank. ■ Distribute money. ■ Collect and count money. ■ Deposit gate receipts.
1 day after	■ Thank all donors and contributors. ■ Make notes for event evaluation. ■ Rest and recover.
2-4 weeks after	■ Meet with committee for comment session. ■ Finish all budget paperwork. ■ Calculate profit or loss.

5

Chapter
FINANCIAL MANAGEMENT

"There are so many things that small organizations can spend a lot of money on if they're not careful," warns one conference coordinator. "Something as simple as coffee: A group decides, 'Oh, we want coffee all day long, because we want to be hospitable.' So they say to the hotel, 'We want a coffee stand somewhere all day long.' The hotel says fine, of course. At the end, they'll discover that they just spent $6,000—on coffee and cold drinks."

Your budget is the final arbiter of all your plans for the event. Its size will determine the site you choose, the food you serve, and the prizes you award. An accurate (and conservative) budget is your best insurance against financial disaster. Always work out your "breakeven" budget first (the event income paying for the event costs), then add in profit needed for fundraising projects.

Never mix event money with your own. *Never* sink large sums of your own money into an event; get an advance from the organization instead. Start a separate bank account for the event or use your organization's official bank account. All checks for incoming monies should be made out to the name of the organization, and your group's treasurer can sign and deposit them.

Organizing Your Budget

Your budget evolves from a working estimate to a final budget that must be documented with your actual receipts and accounting in the manager's report. Contact your organization's treasurer for internal regulations and recommendations on accounting, especially for national and fundraising events. Your organization may already have a system for its financial reports; it will be easier all around if you follow it.

For example, one event listed 100 separate "expense classes" (signs, electrician, refunds, storage, parking, and so forth) in 10 separate categories (including food and entertainment, transportation, personnel, and facility). You may choose to allocate the budget by committee (registrars, refreshments, etc.) or by type (service, person, goods). You may need only two divisions, food and other. If your organization doesn't provide a budget structure, develop a system that lets you see at a glance how expenses and income are shaping up.

For repeat events, look at past budgets for ideas and estimates. Don't just accept them at face value, though. For example, the Southwestern Association on Indian Affairs organizes the annual Indian Market every August in Santa Fe, New Mexico. Recently, the Santa Fe City Council voted to raise the site fees from $5 to $25 per booth. The association protested but eventually gave in. The higher site costs were passed on to the exhibitors, whose per-booth rate changed from $75 to $100.

Expenses

The focus of your event—the banquet, the play, or whatever—is usually the primary expense. At fairs and bazaars, the primary expense is usually the site and raw materials for the merchandise. The prize list may well be your biggest expense at amateur sporting events. The publicity costs for any event open to the public will be a substantial proportion of your budget. If you own the site and/or don't serve refreshments, your major budget proportions will change considerably. Secondary expenses include prizes, decorations, printing costs, purchase of paper goods, and other miscellaneous costs. These will vary depending on the type of event.

A Quick Guide to Budget Proportions	
Food-Focused Event	
Site Fee	20% - 35% of total budget
Food Costs	60% - 75% of total budget
Misc. Costs	10% - 15% of total budget
Non-Food Event	
Site Fee	50% - 75% of total budget
Misc. Costs	25% - 50% of total budget

Site The site fee is a straightforward expense. Many churches, schools, or other institutions charge a flat rate. Some add hourly charges for amenities such as heat or custodial service; some levy individual fees for each room you use or for the use of equipment (tables, chairs, dishes, pianos). Include a breakdown of these costs in your budget. If you own the site, contribute some portion of your event budget to the building maintenance fund.

Refreshments The food cost, though often the largest piece of your budget, is also the most flexible. Here's the best opportunity to inflate or deflate the price of the total event. A banquet featuring chicken instead of beef will keep the price lower; serving lamb rather than beef will raise the price. Remember complementary food items: you listed bread as a budget item, but did you include butter? Don't forget to add in tax and gratuities where applicable.

Publicity Publicity costs (artist fees, printing, photocopying, and postage) form a category by themselves. Classy or expensive events will frequently devote a large chunk of the budget to engraved invitations, four-color posters, and other such items.

Decorations Decorations are a major category for theme events; you can spend a lot on floral arrangements, complicated lighting, and other expensive ornamentation to achieve an authentic atmosphere.

Programming Each activity you plan increases your expenses. Suppose your theatre group presents a play. Do you need to pay for props, costumes, or programs? Or suppose you plan an art display. Does your organization's inventory include bulletin boards and stands, or were they lost so you need to buy new ones? Say you want the musicians to perform special music. Do you need to pay copying costs for sheet music? For example, the budget for the Marlboro Road Race in Marlboro, Massachusetts, included these indispensable programming items: entrant number badges and pins, and fees for officials and marshals. All of these expenses add up. So, check with the appropriate people and take these costs into account.

Prizes Prizes can be a relatively minor expense, and considered part of the programming portion of the budget. The prize budget for sporting events, however, can represent the largest chunk of the budget. Allocate your total prize budget unevenly into prize categories (a common pattern is: first prize, 50%, second prize 25%, third prize 15%, and 10% for fourth prize and/or honorable mentions).

Miscellaneous Miscellaneous costs are variable and sometimes the hardest to budget. Be aware of hidden expenses and try to include every expenditure. If any subcategory in miscellaneous becomes more than 10% of the total budget, pull it out and make a new category.

Typical miscellaneous costs include site signage, office supplies, facsimile machine services, and bad debts; simple decorations, such as balloons or candles; paper goods, such as cups, tablecloths, and trash bags; prizes and tokens.

An event should also reimburse workers for incidental expenses (stamps, long-distance phone calls, and the ticket received for being double-parked while unloading the membership brochures). Include a small estimate for these costs, and then keep close track of them. All legitimate expenses should be paid for by the event and not out of the volunteer's pocket. Document these expenses with "petty cash vouchers" (official receipts signed by recipient) and include as budget items.

Never allow anyone to present you with a bill at the event. Don't pay out any money at the event, either. It's too difficult to keep track of such expenditures. (However, "never-say-never" fans may stock an envelope in their event binder for carrying receipts.)

Income

Income from participants and vendors seems fairly straightforward until you look closely. Category and price setting is actually very complicated (unless your organization, like the United States Cycling Federation, determines the fee structure for approved events).

Different price categories are often assigned to senior citizens, children, adults, members, nonmembers, and students. One Model Railroad Club held an open house and charged $2 for adults and $.75 for children, with a maximum $5 fee "per family." Some organizations offer paid staff tickets at cost. And in Commonwealth countries, unemployed workers are often charged lower fees.

Benefit balls frequently sell tickets "by the couple." These and other expensive fundraisers usually set several price levels and make corresponding changes in treatment. For example, "friends" receive just tickets, "patrons" pay double the friend price and attend a preshow as well as the regular event, and "benefactors" pay double the patron price and attend a champagne reception afterwards.

Think ahead. What age is the cutoff for children or senior citizens? How will they prove their age? Will members be required to show a membership card? What about new members whose cards haven't been delivered yet? Will you offer bulk discounts? If so, what's your minimum order?

Allowing guests to charge their reservations to credit cards, for example, means more paperwork, and you will pay a percentage fee to the credit card company. However, the convenience and that paper receipt are often important to conference attendees.

Warning: don't make more work for your registrars without good reasons!

Option-Based Prices Perhaps you want to offer options for a week-long conference (with banquet, no banquet; with lunches, no lunches; with tours, no tours; early arrival, late departure) or a play (reserved seating, general admission, standby).

Do *not* use one category to subsidize another. For example, if you provide informal snacks during the course of the day, don't use the "float" from your evening banquet tickets to cover that cost; the true cost should be reflected in the total price for everyone. "Site

fees" are common for bring-your-own picnics, field days, and some sports events. Site fee means exactly that: the total price of the site divided by the number of people attending.

Time-Based Prices Some events charge uneven prices in an effort to encourage or discourage certain kinds of reservations. For example, many conventions offer discounts to people who reserve ahead for the entire weekend, and charge a high per-day fee for at-the-door attendees. A $10 advance ticket may be advertised as $15 at the door. This higher price will not only provide recompense for the extra trouble you face with at-the-door admissions, but will also be good incentive for early reservations.

Complimentary Admissions It's essential to decide who is entitled to complimentary tickets—performers, presenters, media, sponsors, and so on. Will complimentary tickets offer different levels of service (second seating only, standing room only, etc.)?

Vendors Exhibitors and vendors are frequently members of your professional association. Usually, size and location of booth affect the fees charged, with corner booths being the most expensive. Will you charge for each exhibit staffer or allow two or three "free registrations" per vendor (and allow them free, limited, or no access to the rest of the event)? Do "supplier members" get a discount on booth prices? What about nonprofit organizations? At one community's street fair, the food vendors paid $125 per booth, but the nonprofit organizations paid only $20 per booth.

Sponsors And don't forget other legitimate sources of income, such as ad and souvenir programs (see discussion of "sponsors" and "programs" later in this chapter).

Sale of Items This category is very active in the budgets of fairs, bazaars, and auctions. Balance your volunteers' skills against your audience's expectations when making pricing decisions. For example, if all merchandise is priced in flat dollar amounts or increments of $.25, giving change is faster and easier, as is the accounting process after the event. On the other hand, marketing psychologists claim that a price of $4.99 is more attractive than a price of $5.00, and that bulk discounts increase sales. Include the sales tax, where applicable, in the price, so that your salespeople don't have to figure it out for each item. (Pricing principles are also discussed in Chapter 13, Entertainments.)

Category Titles   Event managers frequently agonize over category titles. Most agree you can't use "spouse" or "junior member" so freely these days. Suggested alternatives include "guest," "accompanying person," "significant other," "companion," or "associate participant." Work out in advance whether this designation includes same-sex partners.

An Alternative System   Of course, you could always employ the strategy that the Society of Friends uses for lunches after prayer meetings. Quaker Elizabeth Claggett-Borne explains, "We ask people to donate a dollar or two when they come through the buffet line. We don't make a big deal out of it, but the basket is there." Those baskets usually amass enough profit every few months for the group to donate a few hundred dollars to nearby shelters and meal programs.

Preliminary Budget

Do a rough estimate of your budget as soon as your event is conceived. You will already have an idea of the type of event you would like to manage. Once your event has been approved, plan in depth and construct a working estimate of your budget. (Use the budget worksheets in this chapter.) The procedure is explained in detail in the following paragraphs. If you can access spreadsheet software, use it; you can plug in alternatives without losing your original figures.

Estimate Attendance   Check with others who have managed or attended a similar event in recent years. If this is not possible, think about whom this event will attract; is it strictly a local event with 30 to 40 attendees, a regional event with 75 to 150 guests, a full-fledged national event with several hundred people, or an international conference with more than 1,000 participants? Establish a range of attendance, and estimate a figure toward the low end of that range. Be conservative. It is easier to expand plans later than to cut back.

Some organizations routinely provide complimentary registrations for national officers, special guests, or performers. Subtract the estimated number of "comps" to get the estimated number of *paying* attendees.

Estimate Maximum Site Fee   If the site has already been chosen, you should know the fee. If not, use your best estimate.

Estimate Food Costs   Use the estimate from the caterer or hotel banquet manager. Or, if your volunteers will be preparing the food, do it yourself by estimating the cost of your tentative menu. Find out the cost per unit of the basic foods you wish to serve (use regular prices prevalent in the area). Multiply these prices by the amount needed to feed the estimated attendance. Total all food costs.

Add All Other Categories   Don't forget to include expenses such as performance fees, supplies, telephone bills for long-distance calls, gas, and postage.

Add Twenty Percent   Leave some elastic in your budget, advises Hannah Roberts, co-director of the Commonwealth Vintage Dancers in Massachusetts and former alumni relations director. "There are always unexpected expenses. Try to put an administrative line in the budget that will allow for last-minute items that you hadn't anticipated." She speaks from experience. "I figured an instructor was going to use a particular mode of transportation from a particular city, and it turned out that she was going to be coming from somewhere else and needed to come in a more costly manner."

So add an additional 20% to the estimated total expenses to prepare for increases in food prices, unforeseen problems or emergencies, and oversights in your original budget estimate. The extra 20% is the built-in flexibility that a good budget requires.

Total All Expenses   Total all estimates above.

Calculate Ticket Price   Divide the total expenses by the estimated paying attendance figure to obtain a cost per person. (Don't forget to calculate each price category separately.) This is your breakeven figure (for events without sponsors or vendors). Round this cost per person to the nearest reasonable price. For example, if your per-person cost comes out to $8.79, a ticket price of $9.50 or $10 per person is reasonable, if you are not running a fundraising event. A ticket cost of $9 per person allows scant margin for error, so be prepared for the possibility of losing money on the event. A fundraising event might charge anywhere from $30 per person and up, for a profit of $20 or more on each ticket.

Calculate Total Expected Income   Multiply cost of tickets or vendor booths by the expected attendance in each category. Multiply program ads by number, size, and cost. Add totals together to reach a total expected income.

Calculate Profit or Loss The difference between the total estimated cost and the total expected income is the estimated profit or loss from the event. Remember, in some organizations, managers of national events must share profits (in some designated proportion) between the local host group and the national headquarters.

Actual Budget

Your final budget is a more precise version of your working budget. Once the site has been chosen and the actual site fee is known, the menu has been finalized with actual food costs calculated, and performers have signed contracts, your estimates can be replaced by actual documented costs. If your working budget was a good one, actual costs should not differ from your estimates by very much. Ideally, actual costs will be less in some areas so that a small surplus will cover other overrun costs.

Attendance Estimates The main factor affecting the accuracy of your profit or loss forecast is the attendance estimate. Use the attendance figures from past events as a base figure. As reservations come in, you will be better able to determine the actual attendance. At the close of advance reservations, count up all reservations. Add in a reasonable percentage for at-the-door attendance (if allowed at your event). If this figure differs significantly from your original estimate, adjust your budget accordingly. (Read your catering contract carefully to note when final attendance figures are due to the caterer and how much leeway you enjoy for last-minute changes.)

For example, for the last three years, your "Meet the Candidates Brunch" drew between 5%-15% at-the-door attendees. You estimate 100 in attendance; at the close of reservations, you count 75 reservations. Calculating the margin gives you a final figure of 80-85 guests. You may wish to cut back slightly in some areas of your purchases for the event.

Or, at the close of reservations, you count 92. Adding the margin gives you 95-105 guests. Your original estimate stands.

Or, at the close of reservations, you count 103. Adding the margin gives you 110-120 guests. You will need to purchase extra refreshments and supplies.

There are alternatives to playing this last-minute guessing game with attendance and costs. You may publicize that reservations must be made and paid in advance with no at-the-door admittance allowed. You may also admit people at the door on a no-food basis only. Or, limit the total number of tickets so that you will be assured of serving no more than a specific number of guests. (But in all these cases, you still run the risk of falling short and having to cut back.)

Devise a contingency plan in case of unexpectedly high attendance. Bring cash to the event in case you need to send someone to the nearest store for more supplies. This sort of unexpected expense requires a little flexibility in your budget. Otherwise, any emergency could send you plummeting into bankruptcy.

Profit (Is Not a Dirty Word)

That "nonprofit organization" tag does not mean that your event must lose money or just break even. It does mean you should plan for reasonable profits. Of course, if you are running a fundraising event, you'll try for higher profits.

For average non-fundraising events, a built-in profit of 15% to 30% of your total budget figure is reasonable. When costs per person are estimated at $8.79 and you charge $10 for reservations, the $1.21 difference is your "profit" (14%). The event may not turn out as you anticipate: attendance might be low at the event and so you just break even; or more people might attend than expected and your profit is larger. These things are not really under your control. But don't purposefully plan large profits into the budget of a non-fundraising event or you'll warp the goal of the event.

Fundraising Many organizations depend on fundraising events for financial support. For example, the profits from your women's club annual field trip may fund club activities for the entire year. Or, your organization might run a show or exhibition where the largest segment of guests is the general public, and all profits will be channeled back into local organization activities for the year.

Make sure that your estimated profit from fundraising events is worth the effort of sponsoring the event. A rule of thumb is that such events should gross three to four times their cost (if your costs are zero because of sponsors, you'll end up making more than that).

Some fundraising volunteers advocate a kind of "top-down" method of budgeting an event. In this system, you first decide exactly how much money the organization needs to raise; then you plan an event. Fix the admission price per person by calculating actual event costs plus the total profit needed divided by the expected number of attendees. But be aware that events planned in this fashion can reflect their primary purpose all too clearly.

Sponsors

"As a former chamber of commerce manager and current board member for a community foundation, I can attest to the generosity of small businesses in responding to almost daily solicitations by local charities, athletic, cultural, and youth organizations, and service clubs, to name a few," writes Debra Strong in a letter to the editor of *Inc.* magazine. Her view is supported by a government survey which found that 86% of businesses donate materials, services, or use of their facilities to nonprofit organizations, and 76% lend personnel. The International Events Group maintains and distributes listings of sponsorship opportunities for corporations. Use their publications to invite sponsors for your event (see Resources).

Although coordinating several different sponsors seems like a lot of work, using only one sponsor leaves you vulnerable to last-minute pullouts.

Choosing Sponsors Carefully match prospective sponsors to the event. In Pennsylvania, the American Heart Association's ten-kilometer Turkeywalk is partially sponsored by Wampler-Longacre, maker of chicken and turkey products. Walkers receive turkeys and company T-shirts.

Find out what kind of sponsorship most appeals to the company. The most common agreement provides that you name the sponsor in all of your publicity. (For a very high-ticket sponsorship, you'll combine the name of the company with the name of the event.) Be creative. High-profile projects with tangible results are most enticing. For example, General Foods agreed to be a sponsor at the Half Moon Bay Art and Pumpkin Festival in California. Participants received a free face-painting for each empty can of International Coffees.

One conference organizer negotiated two contributions at once. The company sponsored a buffet reception for one night of the conference and provided a knowledgeable employee to present a lecture. "For us, it was interesting because this guy knows what he's talking about and could address these issues. It was

beneficial for him because he got to show off how much he knew, and, in fact, might have signed up some customers . . . So it was a good reciprocal relationship."

Timing Pat Morgan, development officer at Saint Andrew's School in Bethesda, Maryland, gives this tip: "When you solicit, use good timing. Most companies budget an amount for this sort of expense, so ask at the right time, before they've spent it all or promised it all somewhere else." Apply at the beginning of the company's fiscal year (almost always January, sometimes July).

Contracts As always, write a letter of agreement and get it signed by both organizations. When asking vendors to donate goods or services to a nonprofit organization, give any contributors the organization's tax-exempt IRS number for their records. Also apply this number when purchasing taxable items to keep costs down.

Programs Advertisements or "sponsor lists" are often lucrative fundraisers in programs. Determine sponsor categories and costs of ads in advance. Maybe you could try Pat Morgan's method. For an auction at Saint Andrew's School, she thought of a new twist: "We asked businesses to sponsor a page in the program. The business got a one-line credit at the bottom of the page and we had descriptions of auction items on the rest of the page. It was very classy looking."

When soliciting, advise potential contributors of the number and kind of people expected at the event, the theme, and the programming. Show them what they will receive in return for their sponsorship. Bring a "dummy" (a sample program) to display during your conversation. Usually, sponsors and advertisers receive complimentary tickets.

Taxes

There are two sorts of taxes you must worry about: tax forms filed by your organization, and tax forms filed by your contributors. The best advice about U.S. tax regulations is to check with your local Internal Revenue Service agent. Obtain proof of your status as a nonprofit organization (regulated under tax code 501). And, arm yourself with these official publications from the IRS:

■ 557—Tax-Exempt Status for Your Organization
■ 561—Valuation of Donated Property

- 598—Tax on Unrelated Business Income of Exempt Organizations
- 1391—Deductibility of Payments Made to Charities Conducting Fund-Raising Events

Tax-Exempt Activities   In certain circumstances, some of your event income must be carried separately on the organization's books because it is considered "unrelated business income" and is therefore taxable. Some conventions and conferences must make this distinction, depending on exhibitor income and event activities. If you're particularly worried about the tax status of an event, you can get a ruling in advance from the national bureau of the IRS (see Resources).

Deductions for Donors   In his book *The Non-profit Economy*, Burton A. Weisbrod notes, "In the United States, income tax deductibility is used to encourage donations. In the United Kingdom, by contrast, there is no tax deductibility for charitable donations. Donations are, however, partially matched by governmental grants to the recipient organization."

There *are* some federal tax regulations that are fairly clear. The Council of Better Business Bureaus explains: "The price of participating in a raffle or similar drawing cannot be deducted as a charitable donation . . . The purchase price of tickets to a fundraising dinner, circus, or other meal or entertainment event is not fully deductible. Only the portion of the ticket price above the value of the meal or entertainment can be deducted for income tax purposes." Many organizations simply print "tax-deductible to the full extent of the law" on tickets for fundraising events, which is either ducking the question or purposely misleading. Either print the amount of donation (and therefore deduction) on the ticket or don't print any reference to tax deduction. Be responsible.

Being Thrifty

Always make use of the resources of your organization. Ask around; some local members may be eligible for discounts just by being students or employees or by belonging to a food cooperative. Borrow, borrow, borrow—from your members, from your sponsors, from your site. Rent, don't buy, expensive equipment. Ask for used items from businesses that are relocating or closing. Try barter if you are truly desperate.

If money is tight, minimize the cost of extras. Substitute a less expensive dish in one course, or pick your own "free" greens for centerpieces. Or find unusual sources: chairs rented from churches, synagogues, and funeral parlors are cheaper than "party chairs" from commercial suppliers.

Keep an eye on during-the-event expenses. Buy your beverages on consignment, and ask bartenders to open bottles as needed so you can return unused beverages for credit.

Obtain competitive bids, and negotiate price on everything. New business owners trying to get established, such as caterers or performers, might exchange free services in return for publicity and recommendations. Employing students or amateur hobbyists always cuts costs. Usually the publicity committee (photographers, artists) can take best advantage of these semiprofessionals.

NAEIR   Take advantage of your nonprofit status. Most 501 organizations—subsection (c)3—are eligible to join NAEIR, the National Association for the Exchange of Industrial Resources. NAEIR acts as an intermediary between for-profit businesses and nonprofit organizations, soliciting and warehousing overstocks, surplus, and discontinued supplies and equipment—all new items. For a reasonable annual fee, member organizations may order items for free, paying only shipping and handling costs. (See Resources.)

Mail Order   Mail-order products can be much cheaper than locally available goods; be sure to order merchandise well in advance. Give the delivery address of your organization or your workplace to ensure receipt.

Printed Materials   Always ask your printer to return or save negatives, masters, and plates; reprints will cost less. When printing more than 100 copies of an item, ask for bulk discounts. Suggest a package deal on all printing for the event. And you'll nearly always save money if you are willing to accept delivery from the printer in a few weeks instead of a few days. (A "few hours" turnaround time is outrageously expensive, so watch those deadlines!)

Special sizes or colors of papers always cost more and take longer to deliver. Thermography is cheaper than engraving. Design flyers and information packets as self-mailers with address panels; under one ounce (up to five pieces of bond paper stapled together with no envelope) can be mailed with one stamp. If you are mailing the same thing to 225 or more addresses, consider using bulk mail. It cuts costs, but you have to sort by zip code.

6. BUDGET WORKSHEET

EXPENSES

Site		$_____
Room and hall fees	($_____)	
Site staff	($_____)	
Heat/air conditioning	($_____)	
Equipment	($_____)	
Tables and chairs	($_____)	
Refreshments		$_____
Food	($_____)	
Alcohol	($_____)	
Linens	($_____)	
Catering fee	($_____)	
Staff and gratuities	($_____)	
Taxes		$_____
Publicity		$_____
Artist or photographer	($_____)	
Photocopying/printing	($_____)	
Postage	($_____)	
Decorations		$_____
Flowers	($_____)	
Candles	($_____)	
Lighting	($_____)	
Balloons, etc.	($_____)	
Paper supplies	($_____)	
Programming		$_____
Performers	($_____)	
Travel, hotel, etc.	($_____)	
Prizes		$_____
Ribbons, plaques	($_____)	
Miscellaneous		$_____
Telephone	($_____)	
Transportation	($_____)	
Photocopying	($_____)	
Postage	($_____)	
Stationery supplies	($_____)	
Facsimile services	($_____)	
For preliminary budgets, add 20%	($_____)	$_____
	Total	$_____

7. BUDGET WORKSHEET

INCOME

Admissions $_____

     (_____ guests @ $_____each) $_____

     (_____ guests @ $_____each) $_____

     (_____ guests @ $_____each) $_____

     (_____ "comp" guests @ $0 each) $____0____

Ad Programs $_____

     (_____ covers @ $_____each) $_____

     (_____ 1/2 pages @ $_____each) $_____

     (_____ 1/4 pages @ $_____each) $_____

Exhibitors/Vendors $_____

     (_____ booths @ $_____each) $_____

     (_____ booths @ $_____each) $_____

     (_____ booths @ $_____each) $_____

Sale of Items $_____

     (_____ items @ $_____each) $_____

     (_____ items @ $_____each) $_____

     (_____ items @ $_____each) $_____

            Total $_____

TOTAL PROFIT (OR LOSS)

Total Income $_____

   minus

Total Expenses $_____

            Total $_____

Chapter **6**
SITE SELECTION

Alice Freer, a particularly creative event manager who runs her own special events business in Washington, D.C., has rented buses, airplanes, and trains for her special events. One bicycle club holds its races in a deserted industrial park early on Sunday mornings. The 1988 National Model Airplane Championships were held, appropriately enough, at the Naval Auxiliary Landing Field in Chesapeake, Virginia.

As soon as you agree to manage an event, you should begin to search for a site. Your organization may always use the same hall or may own a facility, but your event could be better somewhere else, so don't hesitate to shop around. Consider trading facilities with another organization that also needs a change. You'll want to select the site at least six months before the event.

Site Selection Process

- Calculate site budget.
- Outline site needs.
- Create list of all possible sites.
- Eliminate all but about ten sites.
- Call sites for preliminary screening.
- Narrow choices to three sites.
- Visit sites in person.
- Select site.
- Negotiate price, facilities, and personnel.
- Confirm and exchange contracts.
- Pay deposit.
- Draw master site diagram.

Basic Site Criteria

There are four major criteria for selecting a site: location, cost, size, and facilities. Apply each criterion specifically to your event as you estimate the amount of space needed, the budget allotment, and various other requirements. You should outline your needs *before* investigating possible sites. Think about how important each criterion is to your event. Set priorities, but be willing to compromise. This is a useful step even for annual events; you may decide to change sites.

Location "If you're organizing an international conference, take [advantage of] a whole, smaller city," urges Marjorie Carss, a former program organizer of an International Congress on Mathematics Education. "Having the only event occurring there has tremendous advantages because you've got access to all the accommodations and facilities. Also, you're more likely to get government support and local support. I know major cities look attractive and people from other countries want to go to major cities. But everybody has to come through a major city on their way to the conference, so they do get to see a major city."

Evaluate the mobility of your anticipated guests. Do you expect a lot of people coming from far away will drive their own cars? Or are you running a small event in a town of students without cars? Parking should be plentiful in the former case; public transportation should be easily accessible in the latter instance. Where available, shuttle-bus services and horse-drawn carriages can make sites more accessible.

Another consideration is the proximity of the site to other activities. It is hard to maintain a theme atmosphere if the field abuts on a busy four-lane highway. On the other hand, for public events that depend on "opportunity trade" (voter registration drives and street fairs, for instance), a bustling shopping center is ideal.

Cost The total site cost includes room charges, kitchen fees, equipment rentals, and on-site personnel fees. Police and fire officers, catering licenses, and heat and air-conditioning surcharges are often hidden site costs—don't be unpleasantly surprised. At hotels and convention centers, there may be charges for the facilities manager and other service staff as well as built-in gratuities. Note too that outdoor sites are usually cheaper than indoor sites.

Don't pay setup fees for the tables and chairs when your volunteers can do the task. Free labor is one of the pluses of volunteer organizations, so use your workforce to cut costs.

Size Estimate the size of the rooms and kitchen necessary for your event. Mentally plot areas for specific activities; for example, if you plan to ask actors to perform, you will need a stage area and changing rooms.

A successful annual event will probably outgrow its site every few years. Move *before* the guests feel the space squeeze. On the other hand, a hall that is too large for the number of guests will make your event look under-attended, so an extra-large site may not be a bargain.

Multiply room dimensions (length times width) to obtain the square footage of the room. Don't trust the hotel's set figures (number of people per room); footage allowed per person varies drastically from hotel to hotel. Irregularly shaped rooms and pillars will cut down on usable space. Here's a chart to help you figure the space you need.

Room/People Proportions

Setup	Square Feet per Person
Theatre/Auditorium	9-10
Stand-up Buffets	8-10
Receptions	8-10
Sitting Banquets	10-14
Classroom	15-16

As a guide, a 50′ by 30′ rectangular, unobstructed hall will comfortably hold 150 people seated for a speech and for the stand-up buffet or reception afterwards; or 100 to 120 people at a sit-down banquet; or 90 people in a classroom setting (seated at only one side of the tables).

Booth space for exhibits is set at about 225 square feet for a 10′ by 10′ booth. (This allows for aisles and cross-aisles; don't skimp.)

You set the cutoff figure for participants at your event, but realize that an annual meeting will attract many more people than a local seminar. Be flexible. If you find the perfect site but it's just a little too small, maybe you should plan a 125-person event instead of a 150-person event. Or perhaps you could change your sit-down dinner plans to a buffet reception arrangement.

Facilities If the banquet is the focus of your event, the kitchen facilities are the focus of your site search. If you plan dancing at your event, the site's sound system must be adequate, or you'll need to rent and install proper speakers (and your costs will rise accordingly).

"Adelaide [South Australia] was ideal," according to Marjorie Carss, "because it had the University, Institute of Technology, and College of Advanced Education next to each other on one campus across the street from the city. We had first access to all the University and College dorms and were able to make block bookings at central hotels at very good rates. The South Australian government gave a tremendous amount of support. The city was even prepared to put up signs. And you could just walk across the street to do your shopping."

Selection

Develop a long list of possible sites, using every possible resource. In the telephone book, look under "Churches," "Halls," "Function Rooms," and "Banquet Rooms" for indoor sites with kitchen facilities. Sites for outdoor events such as picnics and fairs can be found listed under "Playgrounds and Parks" and "Recreation Centers." Hotels are worth considering, especially if the event is longer than one day. The International Association of Conference Centers, the International Association of Auditorium Managers, and the International Facility Management Association will give you lots of information and suggestions (see Resources).

Call your local chamber of commerce for local events, or the convention and tourist bureau in states you're considering for national conferences. The Pennsylvania Convention Bureau maintains a computer database of more than 700 sites located throughout the state. In Washington, D.C., search for a copy of *Unique Meeting Places in Greater Washington*. Or, order the book *Places* that film people use. (See Resources.)

Here's a list of sites that creative event managers have used recently:

- Airports (Union County Airport, Marysville, Ohio)
- Aquariums (Monterey Bay Aquarium, Monterey, California)
- Arboretums (Tyler Arboretum, Lima, Pennsylvania)
- Beaches (Huckleberry Beach, Coeur d'Alene, Idaho)
- Boats (*The Cherry Blossom*, Alexandria, Virginia)
- Breweries (Miller Inn, Milwaukee, Wisconsin)
- Campgrounds (Cooper's Lake, Butler, Pennsylvania)
- Caves (St. Peter's Grotto, Antakya, Turkey)
- Country clubs (Moskogee Country Club, Moskogee, Oklahoma)
- Estates (Burghley House, Stamford, England)
- Gardens (Missouri Botanical Gardens, St. Louis, Missouri)
- Lakes (Struble Lake, Honey Brook, Pennsylvania)
- Libraries (Folger Shakespeare Library, Washington, D.C.)
- Mansions (Winchester Mystery House, San Jose, California)
- Mountaintops (Mauna Kea, Hawaii)
- National parks (Rebild National Park, Aalborg, Denmark)
- Plantations (James River Plantations, Virginia)
- Public halls (Departmental Auditorium, Washington, D.C.)
- Rivers (Wabash River, Lafayette, Indiana)
- Sports stadiums (Astrodome, Houston, Texas)
- State parks (North Bend State Park, West Virginia)
- Tents (Festival Tent, Pittsburgh, Pennsylvania)
- Theaters (World Theater, Saint Paul, Minnesota)
- Wharves (Chubb's Wharf, Mystic Seaport, Connecticut)

Keep open to the possibilities. Maybe you could use a farm, island, lighthouse, marina, museum, planetarium, shopping mall, stadium, theme or amusement park, vineyard or winery, or even a zoo.

A Conference Board Survey of more than 900 businesses in Canada revealed that 61% of respondents allowed outside use of their facilities, including rooms, grounds, and vehicles. Bank, government, and office buildings sometimes allow organizations to use their facilities for a minimal charge. Members of college communities may be able to procure an inexpensive campus site for you. Check out the local high schools and private schools, and ask members with children in school to investigate possibilities. Schools are empty during Christmas and Easter holidays, when churches are at their busiest.

Accommodations   Overnight accommodations are sometimes casual (Boston Marathon runners are placed with volunteer families in nearby homes) and sometimes complex (large conferences assign participants to many different hotels). Being honest about the quality of accommodations in advance will save you from angry evaluations after the event. Select housing as close together as possible, and as close to main event activities as possible. Dormitory rooms offer inexpensive housing for conferences during vacation and summer periods. About 400 Dukakis campaign workers were assigned rooms in Emory University during the 1988 Democratic National Convention in Atlanta.

Shorten Your List   Decide what is essential for the site of your event and what you are willing to compromise on. International conferences frequently require simultaneous translation devices, for example, and a site without them cannot be considered. Cancel the chess tournament at the town picnic, maybe; serve a cold buffet at the razzle-dazzle annual meeting, never.

Preliminary site selection requires a telephone and some blank site surveys like the one provided in this chapter. On the telephone, eliminate obviously unsuitable sites: Is this one too expensive? Is that one too small? Are the kitchen facilities adequate for the menu? Will the dressing rooms be suitable for a costume ball? For a dance party, note that dancers generally prefer a wooden floor; a site with concrete floors is a bad choice for such an event.

Narrow your choices to approximately three sites that are available on your chosen date.

Site Visits   The next step in finding the perfect site is personal reconnaissance. When you're playing in the big leagues and scouting out a distant city for a large conference, these visits are known as familiarization trips, or "fam trips." Make appointments to see the sites. Bring along blank site surveys to fill out as you look at each site. And bring or mail an organization brochure so the officials there can learn about your organization. If approval is needed from a town or parish committee, leave the brochure there for their next meeting. The next time you want to rent the site, you'll be able to say "We're in your files," even if the original contact person is no longer at the site.

Ask for or draw up a floor plan with accurate measurements. Don't be afraid to ask questions to ensure that the site meets your needs. Fully explore the possibilities of the site. Are the grounds available for free? One enterprising event manager was able to avoid the usual banquet room of the hotel for luncheons; instead, he discovered and bargained for the elegant, intimate hotel restaurant, usually open only for dinners.

Check out the facilities of each prospective site (inside and outside). There are some unglamorous but very necessary facilities that must be examined. Is there a convenient spot for locating the registration and check-in tables? Cold weather events will require coat check facilities; a hundred coats cannot be piled on a table. Restrooms for both sexes must be evaluated—don't hesitate to look into the facility for the other sex. (At least two stalls per 100 people is recommended.)

Acoustics Glass makes sound bounce, but heavy carpeting or draperies absorbs sound. High ceilings can produce bad acoustics, which accounts for the incredible din in many exhibit halls.

Kitchens Realize that many halls that could easily *seat* 200 people don't include kitchen facilities to *feed* 200 people. Don't assume: a kitchen may feature sixteen burners, but only eight of them may be functional. When the kitchen is a long way from the banquet room, your hot food will probably be cooler when served than you intended. Make sure that everything works before you rent the site.

Outdoor Sites For outdoor events, the ideal site has a dry, level field with available shade and without large rocks or numerous small ones, tree roots, or gopher holes. You may be forced to settle for whatever field is the closest to the hall.

Special features are needed for certain events. For example, for outdoor plays and performances, determine where the sun will be and what are the natural acoustics.

No restrooms near the field means that you'll need to rent portable ones—another expense for the budget.

When selecting a site for an outdoor event, don't just accept the owner's statement that the meadow has never been flooded; visit it the day after a heavy rain. Keep seasonal attributes in mind, too. If your event is in a cold climate, research what those leafy trees are hiding now that will be all too evident during your January event. Blackflies, mosquitoes, or other pests are the scourge of outdoor events in some areas.

To ensure that outdoor events go smoothly, you'll need to check specific laws and regulations with site and local authorities:

■ Size and location of individual campsites
■ Fire safety regulations (and where firewood gathering is permitted)
■ Drinking water supplies
■ Swimming and lifeguards, where applicable
■ Restroom facilities (some states regulate the minimum number of facilities per person)
■ Food regulations (especially important if groups or individuals plan on selling food)
■ Shelters and/or rain dates

Can't find a suitable site? Make your own, as members of Stanford University did. Since there's no beach on campus, seventy-five tons of sand had to be trucked in for a "spontaneous" beach party. The principal activity was the undirected creation of an eighteen-foot sandcastle, complete with gargoyles.

Problems ("Let's Get Drunk and Burn the Building Down")

Alcohol can be a delicate issue when renting a site. Find out the municipal and site regulations for liquor consumption. As at many colleges, student organizers at Rice University in Texas must register any event that includes alcohol with campus officials. Few if any churches will allow hard alcohol to be consumed on the premises. Catholic, Congregational, and Unitarian churches almost always allow beer and wine, but you must ask permission. Usually, Baptist churches prohibit all alcohol.

Fire Codes Find out the fire code for the site. All buildings are authorized for a specific capacity by the local fire regulations. Some sites may provide a "fire marshal"—for a fee.

Insurance and Liability Insurance is a key issue these days. Exchange copies of insurance policies

8. SITE SURVEY FORM

Site name_____

Address_____

_____

Contact_____ Telephone #_____

References (previous events)_____

Total fee $_____ Deposit $_____

Reserve _____ months in advance. Deposit due _____ months in advance.

Fire law maximum capacity _____ people

Alcohol restrictions_____

Kitchen facilities_____

_____

_____

Kitchen equipment_____

_____

A-V equipment_____

_____

Electrical equipment_____

_____

How many tables?_____ How many chairs?_____

Main hall_____

_____

_____

Extra rooms/space_____

_____

Atmosphere_____

Restrooms_____

Public telephone (location/number)_____

Public transportation_____

Parking_____

Special conditions_____

_____

General comments_____

_____

_____

Researched by_____ Date_____

Attach diagram of site (with measurements).

with the site, and don't needlessly expose your volunteers to lawsuits by choosing an unprotected site. Be especially cautious about the clause which assigns "host liability" for alcohol consumption.

Rules and Regulations Know what the site provides and what you are responsible for bringing yourself. It should be possible to drop off some items at the site the day before the event; arrange this when you confirm the site. Don't overlook the obvious: Who takes out the trash? Where? When? If your volunteers will be trash handlers, where is the dumpster? More than one event manager can look back and laugh at the memory of themselves and several hysterical volunteers, wandering around outside in the dark looking for an ingeniously disguised dumpster.

"There are a lot of regulations that come out of the hotel itself: how much electricity the exhibitors can use, what kind of lighting is allowed, and so forth," notes Terry Phinney. She adds: "Food exhibitors usually want to give out food samples; some hotels will allow that, some won't."

Read and understand the implications of any site rules. The DeCordova Museum in Lincoln, Massachusetts, for example, publishes seven pages of detailed guidelines. "Caterers must be on the approved list" (a short list of five) and "no self-catering or drop-off catering is allowed." Also, "decoration must be limited to tabletop floral arrangements." The Decatur Carriage House in Washington, D.C., also lists three "approved tent companies." "Organizations and individuals cannot sell items on the museum's premises" at the Milwaukee Public Museum in Wisconsin. Some sites only allow union members as setup or food personnel. Regulations can play havoc with your budget and your plans, so don't sign a site contract before researching all the ramifications.

Confirmation

After visiting the possible sites and talking with the people in charge, you've established a good basis for deciding which site you want. Reserve your choice immediately; reserve all additional rooms at the site even if you aren't going to use them, unless this increases your total site cost dramatically. Competing events nearby (hearing the rock concert through the wall during your annual meeting) can be very distracting.

It's a good idea to reserve your second-choice site as a backup at this time. For outdoor events, you'll need either a backup indoor site or a rain date site.

Send a letter of confirmation (signed by you and your chapter president) to the site, with date, times, rooms, and prices detailed. Ask them to sign and return this letter (see the model confirmation letter in this chapter). This letter should include:

- Time, date, day, and place of event
- Type and theme of event
- Fees, expenses, deposits, refunds, cancellations
- Specifics of rooms and facilities
- Names, hours, and duties of site personnel

Keep a copy of this letter, and bring it with you on the day of the event. This saves hassling with on-site staff on the day of the event. One event manager remembers an incident at one of her events: "The janitor insisted we should close down at 10 P.M.—the secretary must have given him the wrong information. Luckily, I had brought my event folder with me. I was able to show him that the letter said 'until midnight,' and he backed right down."

Permits and Licenses Fill out all permits and paperwork with city and state officials. Sales tax requirements change from state to state and sometimes this is handled by someone at the site. Contact traffic and parking offices, if necessary. Send a packet of event information (maps, press releases, schedules, and contact numbers) to the local police station.

Site Liaison Shelley Sommer, currently marketing director at the John F. Kennedy Presidential Library and Museum, recommends, "Find out who's going to be there from the hotel. It's usually not the person you've been working with, because it's a whole different crew nine to five weekdays from the weekend crew."

At church and school sites, the custodian or person who will let you into the site is not usually the actual contact person, so ask for the home phone number in case the person with the key oversleeps. Also, keep in touch with the facility manager during the intervening months; this will prevent mix-ups and accidental rescheduling.

Walk-through The administrative committee and the facilities crew should visit the site about a month before the event to take a tour of the site and its facilities.

9. SITE CONFIRMATION LETTER (MODEL)

The Garden Club, 10 Green St., Maintown, NY 00009   Phone: 555-1212

March 15, 1989

Mr. Staff Secretary
Maintown Recreation Center
10,000 Main Street
Maintown, NY 00009

Dear Mr. Secretary,

I am very pleased to hereby confirm my reservation on behalf of the Maintown Garden Club for use of the Maintown Recreation Center on Saturday, November 11, 1989, as follows:

	Time	Cost	Equipment
Custodian	12 noon - 6 P.M.	$ 60.00	
Durham Hall	12 noon - 6 P.M.	140.00	40 tables, 90 chairs
Ballou Room	12 noon - 4 P.M.	25.00	
Empty room with mirror	12 noon - 6 P.M.	0.00	Coat rack
		$225.00 total	

Kitchen.   As you and I agreed, we shall make limited use of the kitchen: refrigerators, sinks, and counters only. I will arrange for a catering permit with the Town Clerk's office.

Custodian.   The custodian, Mr. Feeney, will unlock the building at noon, and secure the building at 6 P.M. He will be on duty in the secretary's office during the entire time of the event. Mr. Feeney will also remove all trash bags at the end of the event.

Payment.   We will send you a refundable deposit of $100.00 by October 9, 1989. The balance ($125.00) will be paid after the event, by the end of November, 1989. If the event is canceled at any time before November 10, 1989, all our monies will be refunded. If the event is canceled on November 11, 1989, we will forfeit our deposit, but the balance will not be owed.

I am delighted with our choice, and look forward to an exciting "Fall Foliage Festival." Please sign at the bottom and return this agreement to me. Thank you.

Sincerely,

Jane Chairperson

P.S. I would appreciate it if you would list this event on your seasonal calendar of events. I will send a poster for the lobby bulletin board after Labor Day. Thanks again.

Agreed: _____ Date: _____
    Mr. Staff Secretary, for the Maintown Recreation Center

10. FACILITIES MANAGER'S SCHEDULE

Timing	Task
4-12 months prior to event	■ Select site (see Chapter 6). ■ Write directions, make map for program. ■ Give map directions to publicity manager. ■ Recruit setup and cleanup crew members. ■ Print and distribute map to your crews. ■ Discuss needs with performers. ■ Contract for security guards, police, etc.
1-4 months prior	■ Meet monthly with both committees. ■ Finish final stages of site planning. ■ Assign exhibitor spaces and meeting rooms.
1 month prior	■ Meet with crew managers and your committee; walk through site. ■ Confirm all arrangements and contracts. ■ Rehearse performers on site. ■ Collect items from storage. ■ Make signs.
2 weeks prior	■ Meet with both committees. ■ Print and distribute site and table diagrams.
1 week prior	■ Meet with both committees. ■ Arrange table and seat allocations. ■ Give final table/chair counts to site.
1 day prior	■ Use checklists to organize and pack. ■ Pick up keys; transport items to the site. ■ Get some sleep (well, at least try).
EVENT DAY	■ Put up directional signs en route. ■ Announce arrival to site officials. ■ Unpack all equipment, set up site. ■ Clean kitchen and hall. ■ Return all furniture to original places. ■ Pack up supplies. ■ Check entire site for people and items. ■ Sign out with site officials. ■ Turn out lights. ■ Lock up all entrances and exits.
1 day after	■ Take down all outdoor signs. ■ Thank all of your volunteers. ■ Clean and return all borrowed items. ■ Make notes on event evaluation. ■ Rest and recover.
2-4 weeks after	■ Meet with committees for comment sessions.

Chapter **7**

FACILITIES

"Don't fight your site," urges Marion Denby, partner in The Planned Event, a special events business operating in Washington, D.C. "See what the possibilities are, then just work a little, add a little, to bring it out."

Each detail of the physical surroundings contributes to the ambiance of your event. (See Chapter 2, Goals and Themes.) Colorful posters, tablecloths over cafeteria or card tables, and candlelight can do wonders for an event at an unattractive site. Hang decorations along the walls and behind the head table (remember to bring tape, rope, or easels to mount balloons, crepe paper, and signs).

Site Diagrams ("You Forgot to Leave Room for the People")

Claudia Laverty oversees many blood drives for the Northeast region of the Red Cross. She noticed that "each head nurse arranges it differently. There are always the same areas: the registration area, the health history area, the donor beds, and the canteen area. But there's no set pattern, it depends on the site. For example, I was at a blood drive that was being held in a lobby, so they needed a big space in the middle for people to walk through. Off to one side were the beds, and the health history area was on the other side of the aisle."

Setting up a site is mostly a matter of common sense. Locate the light switches, power outlets, ther-mostats, and fuse boxes during your original site tour. Use site diagrams to schedule, predict, and plan. Draw every possible configuration of tables and chairs. (Use the site diagram form in this chapter.)

Sometimes a special event or meeting must be spread among several sites. One event manager advises: "We put those sections which are more popu-lar or have a bigger draw on the so-called fringes fur-ther out. We know that people will be motivated to get there."

You may want to change settings for different event activities, but remember that this will interrupt the timing and crowd movements. At conferences, it's typi-cal to designate the fifteen minutes that it takes for "breakdowns" (dismantling or rearranging the furni-ture) as coffee breaks or loose time to mingle outside the meeting rooms.

Be logical. If the only entrance and exit is a single doorway, don't expect 300 people to empty the main hall in five minutes so that you can set up the tables for dinner.

Practical site layouts allow for easy traffic patterns, busy space, and quiet space. Locate lounge rooms away from the bustle of the main hall. Food concession tables and kitchens are noisy, and should be located away from seminar rooms. A "buffer space" or hallway between the banquet tables and the kitchen will pre-vent loud kitchen noises and harsh fluorescent lights from intruding on a candlelit atmosphere.

Plan the layout of the site in advance. Locate:

Registration area	Kitchen	Stage
Telephone	Restrooms	Dressing rooms
Information table/s	Vendor tables	Banquet tables
Head table	Display area	Coat check
First-aid station	Children's room	Entrances/exits
Elevators	Escalators	Stairways
Sound system	Thermostat	Janitorial closet
Main light switch	Electrical outlets	Lost & found
Supply closet	Fuse box	Dumpster

Copy these diagrams. Give them to crews as site maps.

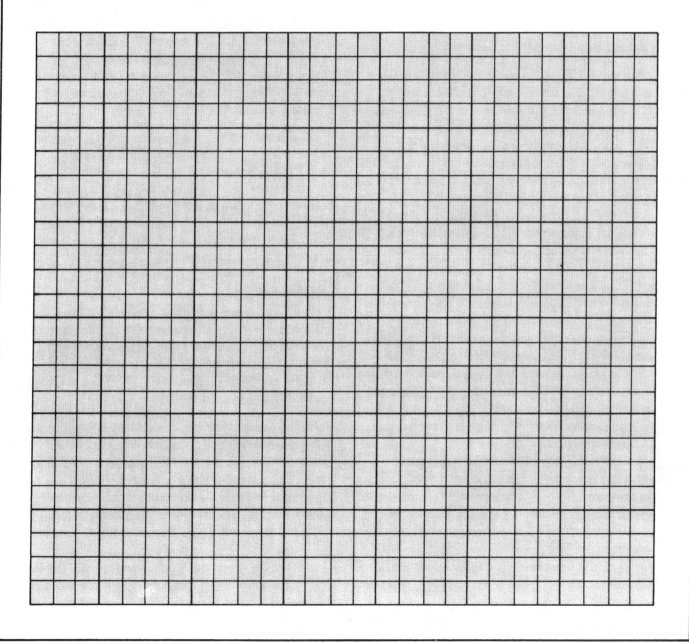

Faced with a standard rectangular room, some meeting managers orient the room from corner to corner, which gives a central area for meeting space and two "breakout" spaces for sessions or exhibits. And this way, no one has to sit at the "back" of the room.

Designate an area where publicity pictures may be taken. Cigarette smoking should be banned or confined to designated areas, as local law dictates.

Exhibitors and Vendors   "We've learned over the years that we cannot separate our exhibitors. That is, we cannot put them in another facility," says Terry Phinney, regional director for the American Camping Association. "For example, some hotels have meeting rooms in the hotel but put the exhibitors off in another building. That does not work for us. People will not walk the distance." Sales demonstrations and the like should be located in high-traffic areas.

Children   Hannah Roberts, co-director of the Commonwealth Vintage Dancers in Massachusetts, echoes the unformulated policies of many small, non-profit organizations: "In general, parents are responsible for their children. We don't prohibit anyone from bringing a child, but we haven't actively provided childcare. Sometimes, we've had teenage daughters present who are willing to baby-sit. We actually have had fairly young children, seven- or eight-year-olds, who have participated in our events. If the interest is there, we've certainly welcomed them."

The entire childcare issue has generated controversy, and special events are not exempt from this problem. The majority of Americans believe that diaper changes and breast feeding should not take place in public; set up a separate room or screened area where parents of either sex can take their children. (Event staff can also advise parents to move children who are creating a disturbance to this room.) Try making a children's corner an "art room": stock it with newspaper, wallpaper, or wrapping paper, and crayons, glue, and decorative beads.

You'll be much too busy managing the event to supervise your own children, so make the necessary arrangements. (Settle in advance whether or not your organization will reimburse your baby-sitter fees.) Some larger cities have day-care businesses that serve conventions and meetings, such as Temporary Tot Tending in San Francisco, California. Don't provide a baby-sitter at the event unless your liability insurance is adequate.

Table Diagrams   Draw up your table and chair layouts in advance, using a rough estimate of how many guests you expect. Measure the tables available at the site.

Table Sizes

Rectangle 5' x 36"	6-8 people
Rectangle 6' x 36"	8-10 people
Rectangle 8' x 36"	10-12 people
Round 42"	6 people
Round 48"	8 people
Round 54"	8-10 people
Round 60"	10 people

Adjust your layout to the size and shape of your hall and tables. (See Table Diagrams in this chapter.) Use the "E" diagram with rectangular tables for maximum seating. The "U" or "X" shape takes up space in a large hall. The "V" is a good layout for audiovisual presentations. Lectures are generally held in "classroom" settings. "Restaurant" layout uses offset rows for maximum seating with round tables.

Vendors   Straight rows, aisles, and cross-aisles are common for bazaars and sales; simply assign booths to vendors and let them arrange within the confines of their space. Or you may ask a hotel or convention center for their standard exhibitor arrangements. In either case, try to avoid rows and rows of booths with similar merchandise or displays. Alternate vendor and exhibitor booths, if possible.

Equipment

Many kinds of equipment are available for meeting managers. The appropriateness of the technology is the single most important aspect of the equipment decision. Does it fit the mood and purpose of your meeting or special event? Budget is, of course, another crucial factor in your decision.

Resources   Equipment may be furnished by you, your organization, the speaker, and/or the meeting facility. When the International Congress on Mathematics Education was held in Adelaide, Australia, overhead projectors, computers, monitors, and other electrical equipment were borrowed from area schools.

Carefully note equipment formats, brands, and sizes. You don't want a presentation ruined because the speaker brings a Betamax videotape—but the conference facility provides only a VHS videotape player. If a presentation will be moved to different locales, keep the equipment simple and choose common brand names to avoid last-minute rental panics. Overseas meeting managers must double-check compatibility of all electrical equipment. Television and video cassette recorders, for example, cannot be converted for foreign countries.

Spare projector bulbs, extension cords, multi-prong converters, and other handy devices can avert disasters. To keep track of sales at fundraising events, you'll need some combination of cash registers, receipt books, item tags or total sheets, pocket calculators, and adding machines. In overflow crowd situations, a closed-circuit television system can be used to expand crowd capacity.

Screens Give careful consideration to your screen material, size, and placement. There are some low-budget methods of making a screen. Screens must be wrinkle-free, seam-free, and white (not cream or off-white). You may use clean white walls, sheets, pasteboard, or canvas.

The best viewing is done from seats that slope down to the screen. The screen must be placed above head level but not at a painful angle. The ceiling must be at least fifteen feet high for sixty or more people in a level room to give adequate screen clearance.

Graphics A common error in audiovisual presentations is small text that is too hard to read. As a rule, the smallest letters should be about three inches high when projected.

Slide and overhead projectors should be smoothly integrated into the presentation; rehearse all speakers beforehand to avoid awkward changes and poor pacing.

Displays and Exhibits For poster sessions or events in which exhibits are the focus, create well-ordered displays. Chicken wire, fishnet, corkboard, and pegboard make good upright presentation surfaces; use paper clips, tape, hooks (even bobby pins in a pinch) to fasten articles. Easels are right for some displays, but don't set them in heavily trafficked areas; people may trip on the legs.

Placement and Testing "Most rental companies just deliver, they don't set up," warns one event organizer. Tape down cables and cords to avoid accidents. Put "locks" on all slide carousels, just in case. All equipment should be checked during setup.

Make absolutely sure that sight lines are open from all parts of the room. Place warning signs, put up rope

barriers, or remove chairs and tables where audio or video reception is poor. Don't line up chairs or tables directly behind each other; stagger furniture to provide better viewing and listening.

If you are depending on audience participation in large lecture halls, provide microphones and be sure they work. You may want to set up some stationary microphones and ask audience members to stand up at the nearest microphone. Panel members should be provided with individual microphones for easy access.

When testing for sound levels, remember that human bodies will absorb sound (and make some of their own). The more people in the audience, the louder and more sophisticated the audio equipment must be. However, in large or echoing halls, a mass of quiet people will improve acoustics.

Equipment that will be used sequentially should be reset between presentations. Be sure to schedule warm-up and cool-off periods if necessary for that particular piece of equipment.

Never turn out the lights completely for an audiovisual presentation. Sharp variations in lighting disorient your audience, and completely dark rooms put them to sleep. Dimming the lights is recommended for best viewing.

Signs

Signs posted in strategic locations are an important element of good organization. Use signs wherever possible to prevent intrusion or eliminate confusion—outdoors and indoors, both en route and at the site. Signs and programs should contain as much information as possible to keep loudspeaker announcements to a minimum.

Making Signs Hotels may supply industrial signage; all you decide is what to say where. At less commercial sites, you'll need to make your own signs. Don't use a professional artist if money is tight. Just print the information in a legible hand, or use large stencils. If you want a fancy border, you can do a lot with the cut-and-paste method. (See Chapter 8, Publicity.)

Or, "blow up" (photocopy and enlarge) a poster, handout, or speaker biography. Use rubber cement to mount the blowup on stiff cardboard. Display this placard on an easel outside the session room or hall. In multi-seminar, multi-meeting situations, project a title slide or graphic (of the upcoming speaker or subject) during the break between presentations. This allows

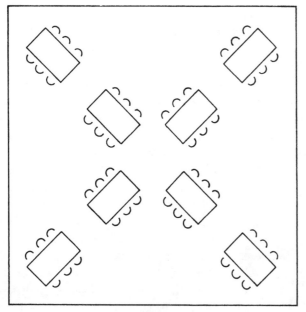

'X' Configuration
8 Short Rectangular Tables
(Seats 48)

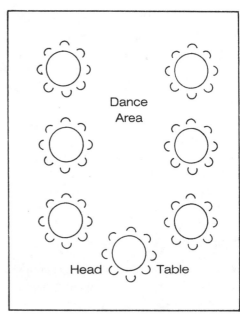

'U' Configuration
7 Round Tables
(Seats 56)

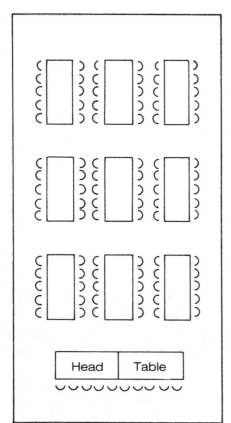

'E' Configuration
11 Long Rectangular Tables
(Seats 100)

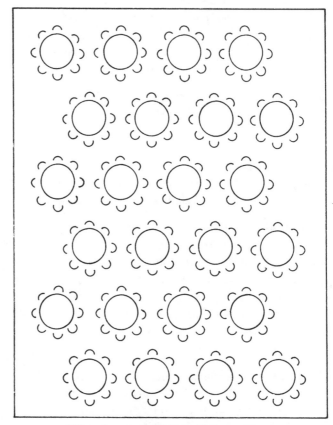

'Restaurant' Configuration
24 Round Tables
(Seats 192)

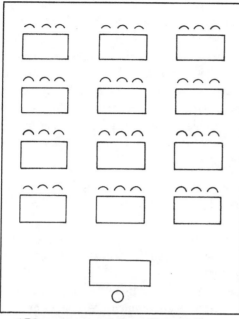

'Classroom' Configuration
13 Short Rectangular Tables
(Seats 37)

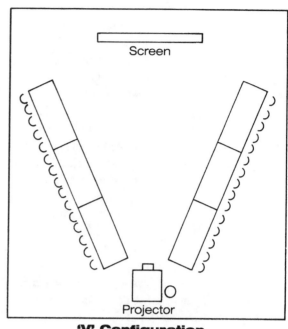

'V' Configuration
6 Long Rectangular Tables
(Seats 30)

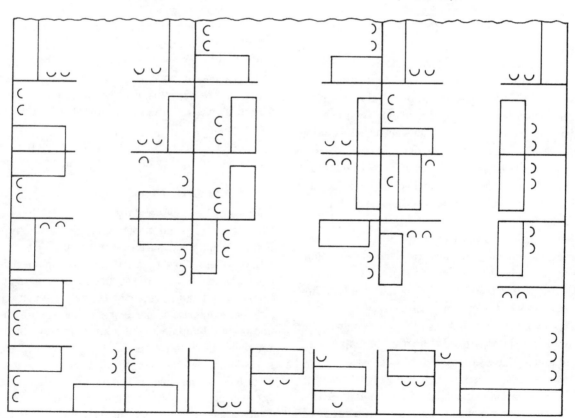

'Exhibit' Configuration
Long Rectangular Tables
(10′ x 10′ Booths)

audience members to identify the right room and seat themselves confidently, avoiding the projection path.

Carol Pierson, an artist for Blue Cross and Blue Shield advises: "Sturdy signs can be constructed of corrugated cardboard or railroad board (which comes in colors). Be prepared for damp weather; use water-proof paint such as enamel or acrylic. Use colors that make good contrast. For example, on dark blue, dark green, or dark red, use a yellow or white paint; on yellow, orange, or white, use a black, brown, or dark blue paint. For after-dark arrivals, use fluorescent tape for your letters." (See Illustration 13A, Signs, in this chapter.) Make all your directional signs the same colors so they will be easier to spot.

Make a master copy of your sign in black on white paper and then make copies on colored paper. Larger signs can be made on railroad board. Letter them with a flat brush (1″ to 1½″ wide) using poster paint or ink, or use large felt-tip markers. All of these publicity and poster supplies are available at art stores.

Placing Outdoor Signs You may need to obtain permission from the police or city officials in order to post signs. In some cities, putting signs on utility poles is prohibited by law.

Before the site opens, see that someone goes over the various routes and posts signs at intersections, confusing forks, and at one or two points along long, unmarked stretches. The signs need only say the organization or event name and show an arrow pointing in the right direction. Use large, oddly shaped signs; triangles and circles are good. Drivers must be able to quickly spot them, read them, and act on the information. Inspect a sample sign from across the street to see if it does the job.

If there are several routes to the site, consider having several of your helpers each travel a different route to put up and take down signs along the way. This will prevent one person from spending all morning traveling different routes to the site in order to place signs. If the take-down person is different from the one who put them up, he or she may need a diagram or map in order to find all the signs.

Outdoor events spread over large expanses must post several location maps of the site with YOU ARE HERE prominently marked. You'll also probably need PARKING, SHUTTLE BUS STOP, and TO THE (*NAME OF EVENT*) signs with arrows pointing in the appropriate direction.

Punch holes in the corners of signs and tie them to poles, trees, or fences with thin rope or strong cord. (See Illustration 13B, Signs, in this chapter.) If you don't know exactly where the signs are to be placed, make the arrows on a separate piece of cardboard and tie or tape the pieces together on the spot in the correct position. (See Illustration 13C, Signs, in this chapter.) This also makes it easier to use signs again for your next event. But remember, tape does not stick in the rain.

Placing Indoor Signs Signs for the hall should be made in advance and posted before the event opens. Post copies of the day's scheduled activities at the registration table and on the grounds; this keeps people from wandering away when you most want them to stick around.

Don't forget nameplates for panelists. Prominently mark the men's and women's restrooms and the room for national officers (if there is one). Be sure to post large and legible KEEP OUT or STAFF ONLY signs if there are restricted areas at the site. If there is a private telephone which is not to be used, put a sign on it. There may be places at the site where people should not take food or drink; again, use a sign. A well-placed and tasteful sign can eliminate many problem situations. Some events may require specialized signs for special-interest groups, craftspeople, or information booths, as well as concession signs that include price lists for food.

Boggled at the vast number of signs you will need? Throw a poster party and get them all done at once!

On the Day of the Event

Unload all supplies and distribute them to the appropriate areas. Post all indoor signs. Set up the registration table and make sure that it is staffed. Install the sound system, move the furniture, set up special areas. In the meantime, the kitchen crew sets up the kitchen and begins preparing the refreshments. Provide entertainers and speakers with adequate space and proper equipment. Put a large message board near the main entrance to the hall. Clearly rope off and post signs for spaces and rooms that are not to be used. (Site officials may charge you for rooms that you did not rent but organization members wandered into.) Deliver one table and two chairs to each exhibit booth. Arrange wastebaskets. Strike a balance between a warm room and a well-ventilated room. In short, do whatever can be done before the guests arrive.

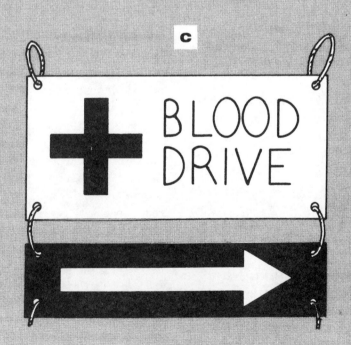

Keep your emergency plans ready if outdoor activities are rained out (long hallways where races can be run; a room for board games and players, etc.).

Outdoor Events   Before setting up for an outdoor event, walk over the field. Check for obstacles and holes. Remove debris. Use the clearest, most level part of the field for physical activities.

Especially in the case of animal exhibitions or any sport with projectiles (horseshoes, javelins, caber toss), spectators must stay well back from the perimeter of the games field. Occasionally, projectile equipment does fly out of bounds, and it can do so with dangerous force. So mark off the playing field or racetrack with posts or stakes about five feet high. Stretch strong twine or thin rope between uprights; then tie small pieces of cloth to the rope to enhance the visibility of the perimeter for participants and spectators alike. A separate "contestants' area" will keep the athletes' equipment in a central location for ease of access and general aesthetics.

Cardboard chairs are a new product on the market. These chairs can support up to 220 pounds. Currently, businesses are using these chairs as a form of advertising—small, portable billboards. Maybe you could get a sponsor to supply this kind of temporary seating for your outdoor event.

Portable toilets should be rented for some outdoor sites, even if indoor toilets are available. One unit per 150 people is about right; if the crowd is mostly female, rent one unit per 100 women.

Prohibitions and regulations should be made clear to all in attendance. Warn people not to walk in the woods alone or swim alone. Post signs to mark trails and clearly define boundaries. Mark areas containing poison ivy or sumac. Fires must be strictly contained. Do not allow torches or open flames inside or too close to tents. Know the site rules about open fires if you are planning to cook outside or sing around a bonfire.

Security

If you think about it, *security* is a wonderful word, and exactly the environment you want at your event. You don't want an armed camp; you *do* want enough preventive measures taken to make your guests feel *secure* as they enjoy the festivities. Managers must either designate a "safe area," kept locked, or must warn guests to keep track of valuables. Signs in coat rooms or restrooms stating "Do not leave valuables unattended" can prevent a sticky situation. And on a personal note, don't forget to arrange for a safe place to keep your own valuables and to lock up the cash box.

Police   The site officials may demand that a certain number of police officers be present during your event. If you are expecting more than 200 people, or if you will be collecting large sums of cash, please take the precaution of contacting the police. Hotels and other businesses may employ a private security force; security coverage would be part of your contract in this case.

Lost and Found   Establish a place for lost and found articles at the beginning of the event. Use a clearly marked box (perhaps placed in the registration area or at the coat check counter); guests can check it as they leave and sign for their own articles.

Courtesy Volunteers   Maintain a congenial atmosphere in the hall with the aid of some chosen helpers. They may be greeters, errand runners, or burly bouncers, depending on the need and the festivities. Consider designating some volunteers to act as co-hosts, helping you with social and crowd control situations and welcoming guests. New members, performers, visiting dignitaries, and other important visitors should be introduced to other people.

Problem People   Unfortunately, people sometimes aren't on their best behavior. Don't hesitate to intervene in unpleasant situations. If someone slips through without paying, quietly ask him or her to pay, or ask security to eject the "crasher." If people are obnoxiously loud, rude, or insulting, ask them to behave and restrain their language. The majority of your guests will appreciate your efforts on their behalf, and the entire event will benefit.

The choice and responsibility of removing a guest from a specific activity or the entire event belongs to the safety or police officer. In cases where there is no official security, draft a crew to act as site security. If you notice someone who has been drinking to excess or who otherwise poses a safety hazard, tell your designated volunteer. If the troublemaker resists, you must take action. Do it firmly but quietly. Avoid making scenes by remaining calm and controlled.

Safety   If you plan to include athletic activities at your event, contact your local Red Cross, hospital, and police. Ask these organizations for safety suggestions and required items. A first-aid kit is a necessity at all events. It's best if safety officers or health personnel are in attendance at athletic events.

Minimum First-Aid Kit

- Scissors
- Medical tape
- Band-Aids
- Stretch and gauze bandages
- Aspirin
- Antacid
- Disinfectant
- Ice packs
- Sunscreen lotion
- Sanitary napkins and tampons
- Insect repellent

Be sure to stop all physical contests before dusk descends, or turn on outdoor field lighting early.

Emergencies   Bomb scares, fire alarms, and other site emergencies are scary situations that require prompt and responsible action. Evacuate the building with the help of safety officers. For large public events, make sure people form a line outside in a safe place. Let people know the cause of the problem (speculation is more frightening than the truth). Estimate and announce how long it will take for the event to get back on track. Send a messenger down the line of people to let them know your tentative restarting time. If possible, pass out refreshments. Let staff and volunteers back on site as soon as the site officials permit. Communicate the revised schedule to your crews, and get everyone ready in place again; then let the crowd back in and continue the event.

Cleaning and Closing the Site ("How Did We Get Crème Caramel on the Ceiling?")

Methods for cleaning up depend on the nature of the event and the facilities at the site. Assuming you enlisted the aid of a capable crew, the following tips should make cleanup easier.

The goal of cleanup is to leave the site in better condition than it was before the event. Even if on-site employees were responsible, you should personally check the entire site at the end of the event to make sure this is accomplished.

Note that bathrooms should never be used for dishwashing, because the food remnants ruin the plumbing and may cost you future use of the site. It's not good hygiene practice, either.

Site Staff   At many sites, a function manager will be assigned to oversee your event. Find out in advance exactly what duties that person will perform. There may also be other staff in attendance, such as janitors, servers, and so on.

At low-cost, low-staff events, attempt to lessen the custodian's burden without being underfoot. Carry trash out throughout the evening, set up tables and chairs (and put them away in the same place), and sweep. Make sure kitchens and bathrooms are spotless and all trash and personal belongings cleared away before you leave the site. You might offer the custodian food and drink and plan a tip for the service in your budget. Chances are the custodian will sing the organization's praises and the site officials will welcome your group back again.

If, however, you are paying the higher prices demanded by many hotels and convention sites, such janitorial services are part of the contract (and the price), so use them to their full extent without feeling guilty.

Procedures   Once servers have cleared the last of the dishes, the cleanup of the banquet hall begins. Announce centerpiece giveaways, award door prizes, then declare the end of the meal. At informal picnics and the like, place several trash barrels in strategic locations.

If other activities will follow in the same hall, tables and chairs must be removed quickly. Crews of three (one person with sponges and two movers) should remove chairs, wipe off tabletops, and fold and store tables. Do a quick sweeping of the floor before turning the hall over to new festivities. As the event continues, finish the kitchen cleanup, take out the garbage, and distribute leftovers.

If after-dinner activities take place in a different space, the same cleanup chores may be done more leisurely and only one thorough sweeping may be necessary.

After the event activities are finished, replace any furniture or items that were moved during the event. If a great deal of moving was done, refer to your pre-event diagram or list for displaced items and their original locations. Sweep and mop floors thoroughly, and check the hall for refuse and lost items. All other rooms used will require a once-over after the event concludes.

Rotate and Reward   Even if you rotate work crews, cleaning up while others enjoy themselves is an unappealing duty. Show these people your special appreciation: ask the musicians to serenade them or present them with buttons or some other token. This does wonders for morale.

Closing the Site   Clear the hall of everyone except the cleanup crew one hour before your actual deadline. Be gentle but very firm with stragglers; offer to move their bags to the foyer. Turn out lights or close off areas that are already cleaned to emphasize your point. Escort guests to the entryway, smile, and say "Thank you for coming, and goodnight."

Turn off all appliances, audiovisual equipment, ovens, and faucets. Make sure all windows are secured. In most cases, there will be a caretaker or custodian at the site who will turn off lights and lock doors. (Don't forget to thank him or her.) However, if the event manager is responsible for securing the site, make sure that the exact procedure is made clear and arrangements for keys have been agreed upon beforehand.

Before leaving the site, make a final check of the entire facility. Pick up the lost-and-found box and take it home with you. The event manager should be the last person to leave the site.

14. FACILITIES CREW CHECKLIST

Contact list (home and work telephone numbers)
Contracts
First-aid kit
Permits
Schedule
Site diagrams
Site letter

Audiovisual equipment
Black electrical tape
Extension cords
Flashlights
Lights, lightbulbs, gels
Needle and thread
Ropes or other barrier markers
Rubber bands
Safety pins
Spare bulbs
Spare fuses
String/twine
Three-prong converters
Walkie-talkie

Paper
Scissors
Signs
Staple gun
Transparent tape
Wide felt-tip markers

Brooms, mops, and buckets
Hand soap
Paper towels
Sponges
Toilet tissue
Trash bags

15. PUBLICITY MANAGER'S SCHEDULE

Timing	Task
5-12 months prior to event	■ Recruit and meet with committee. ■ Use theme to develop event name and logo. ■ Outline audience characteristics. ■ Publish date in member newsletter calendar.
3-5 months prior	■ Meet monthly with both committees. ■ Figure preliminary budget with treasurer. ■ Ask performers for biographies and photos. ■ Design publicity strategy and materials. ■ Draft press releases, fact sheets, etc. ■ Shoot photos and video PSAs. ■ Ask for bids from printers.
2-3 months prior	■ Meet monthly with both committees. ■ Coordinate program with program manager. ■ Drop off originals at printer. ■ Pick up publicity from printer. ■ Send publicity to organization newsletters. ■ Address and mail invitations. ■ Deliver publicity to external media.
1-2 months prior	■ Meet monthly with both committees. ■ Create ads; deliver with payments. ■ Prepare display windows and on-site banners. ■ Set up windows and banners as permitted.
1 week prior	■ Meet with both committees. ■ Arrange for press tickets; reserve seating. ■ Collect press kits and name tags for media. ■ List media personnel for registrars. ■ Distribute posters.
1 day prior	■ Use checklists to organize and pack. ■ Poster important sites again. ■ Get some sleep (well, at least try).
EVENT DAY	■ Greet media personally. ■ Schedule instant interviews. ■ Take photos. ■ Set up press room with publicity kits.
1 day after	■ Clip all media mentions; send thank-yous. ■ Thank all of your volunteers. ■ Make notes on event evaluation. ■ Rest and recover.
2-4 weeks after	■ Meet with committee for comment session. ■ Implement evaluation techniques.

Chapter
PUBLICITY

Some event managers are convinced that any publicity is good publicity, while others never think of telling anyone except other members about their event. The best approach, of course, lies somewhere in the middle.

It's important to project a consistent image of your event in all publicity. The image and identification of the organization can be communicated via the logo and the theme of the event. Dr. Judy Green, working for the Unitarian Universalist Association, developed the theme "There's Music in the Air" for a continental fundraising concert. She paid $300 for a logo designed around that theme. "We literally had no design problems thereafter," she reports. The logo was prominently displayed on T-shirts, tickets, pledge cards, bags, pins, programs, and advertisements. "Sometimes, if you put the money up front to do that, you save yourself a lot of time and energy—and probably money in the long run. It was the best $300 we ever spent . . . worth about $3,000."

Tap professional associations, such as the Public Relations Society of America or Women in Communications, for help with your publicity and media relations (see Resources). Or sponsor a contest at a local art school for a logo or design scheme.

Scheduling

All publicity should be approved by the chapter president before publication. Two months ahead is the minimum time for publicizing a small local event, and more

lead time is required for a large or regional affair. Advance notice is especially important if you plan contests that require prior preparation, such as costume balls or horticultural competitions. Some organizations send save-the-date postcards months in advance. Send out invitations about two months ahead, and mail them in the middle of the month to avoid the "bill cycle" at each end of the month. Continue publicizing your event right up to the time that you stop taking reservations. If there is no limit to the number of people that you can accommodate, you can publicize up to the day of the event itself.

Audience

The type and goal of your event should identify your audience. For example, Craig Macfarlane, president of the Boston Road Club, knows the audience for his club's annual bicycle race and where to find them. "We announce the event at our weekly training races, we advertise at bike shops (put up posters and leave application forms), and we advertise in bike-racing newspapers."

Are you trying to attract new members? Hoping for some television coverage? Doing some simple fundraising expecting families in the community to attend your Easter Fair? Your goal determines how many people you want to reach and what reaction you want from them (simple recognition of your organization's name, monetary sponsorship, attendance, and so on).

Think about the characteristics of your audience. Be able to identify their gender, age, occupation, income level, and membership status. This portrait should tell you how to reach your audience.

One class reunion organizer advises: "If you call your high school office, they should be able to furnish you with names and addresses of the students at the time of graduation. You can use a phone directory from your old hometown and contact people with the same last names. State that you are planning a class reunion and are trying to contact members. Most people are very cooperative. It is a good idea to advertise in the local paper of a planned reunion."

Decide who you want to hear about your event and what sort of methods you want to use to reach them. Identification of your audience is crucial to productive publicity. Don't waste your publicity efforts—focus your publicity at the most important audience.

Direct Mail

Direct mail is an option for event publicity that allows you to "target" specific groups of people. In the simplest form of direct mail, send an event announcement to each member of your organization, including a ticket order form. (See Illustration 16, Direct Mail, in this chapter.)

Christine Simonsen volunteered her professional talents as an event manager for a fundraiser that the Society of Arts and Crafts co-sponsored with a local arts council. She outlined her strategy this way: "The mailing lists were not purchased; they were developed through our own organizations and our contacts. We did a mailing of 5,000, of which 2,000 were from our own group and 600 from the arts council and other art-related organizations. Also, board members provided lists through alumni clubs, and two other arts galleries gave us a list of customers. So it wasn't just a list of members or contributors to the organizations, it was 'friends' that we had identified. All the lists were coded so we could track each for its effectiveness. The strongest pull was through our two organizations that co-sponsored the event." She mailed out 5,000 invitations and 500 guests attended.

Ask each administrative committee member to make a list of potential attendees (in private, not at a meeting, so your total list will be bigger). Or you can purchase a list of likely prospects, either directly or from a "list broker" (salesperson who sells lists). You'll find information on lists and list brokers in the Standard Rate and Data Service Direct Mail List directory in your library. For example, if you're running a workshop on environmental hazards in the Great Lakes area, you might purchase the subscriber list from *Michigan Natural Resources* magazine. Collate your lists and eliminate duplicate entries.

A common technique, especially for fundraising events, is to divide lists into categories: *A*, *B*, *C* and so on. Send the *A* list out first; then, as declines come in from the *A* group, send out the equivalent number of invitations to the *B* list. When you've exhausted the *B* list, begin on the *C* list, and so forth. Always start from your strongest supporters and work out; it's cheaper and more efficient. Dolly Ladd, of Saint Andrew's School in Bethesda, Maryland, agrees: "We used last year's patron's list as the starting list for this year's event." And, of course, she adds, "If you've got people working on the event, they'll want to come."

Many experts advise event managers to coax committee members into "borrowing" membership lists from other compatible groups that they also belong to. Always ask permission *directly* from the group in question; it's not ethical to steal lists, no matter how much of a "good cause" is involved.

Envelopes "Always order the envelopes first," urges Shelley Sommer, former event manager for the Democratic Governors' Association, "so they are addressed, stamped, and ready to stuff when the invitations are delivered late from the printer—and they *will* be delivered late." The classier and more expensive your event is (or the friendlier the image you want to convey), the more imperative it is that invitations should be hand-addressed and stamped, not metered. This method of personalizing large mailings is extremely time-consuming. Fortunately, in this technological age, you can cheat a bit. Programs such as *Longhand* have been written for personal computers; this software claims to "hand-address" 250 envelopes an hour, which is much faster than any volunteer. For $100, it may be a good investment for your organization.

Use home addresses whenever possible. Print "address correction requested" on the envelope and pay the fee for returned invitations; it's the cheapest way to "clean" your mailing list. And don't forget to ask your post office about bulk mailings (see Chapter 5, Financial Management).

Newsletters: The Hidden Market

Exploit your own organization's newsletter as much as possible, right from the beginning. If it features an event calendar, get your date in as soon as possible,

Copy back-to-back

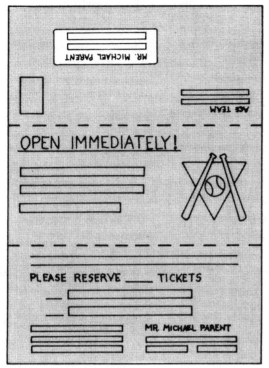

Outside

Inside

Fold

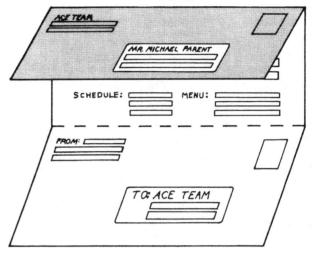

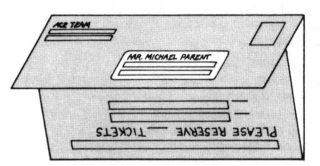

Staple

Front ready to mail

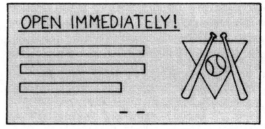

Back ready to mail

even if you don't yet have any other information available.

Compile a list of other newsletters that might feature your event. Almost every one of your volunteers is on a mailing list for an employee newsletter; can they gain access for your event? Perhaps you can even place feature stories (or an interview with the relevant volunteer). Check for special-interest newsletters. Notices of community events can be sent to local school and church newsletters; the smaller the publication, the better the chance that your event will be noticed.

Many organization newsletters allot a certain proportion of total space to each event. Over the stated limit your notice may be considered a "paid internal ad." Check advertising prices, and determine whether or not your event needs extra purchased publicity.

Some publications retype and/or edit all announcements; in this case, make absolutely clear what information can be cut from your notice and what is essential. Most announcements will include the following:

- Name, theme, and logo of the event
- Date and day of the week
- Organization's name
- Menu (for food-focused events)
- Price, deadlines, and address for tickets
- Schedule (doors open, doors close, programming)
- Event manager's name, address, and telephone number
- Site name, address, and telephone number
- An accurate set of directions

Check the requirements of each publication before you create anything. You don't want to go to a lot of trouble only to find your 8½″ by 11″ announcement reduced beyond the limits of legibility in order to make it fit on the page.

Maps   You must include a good map. Give directions for both public and private transportation. Go over the route yourself in a car to check that you have written the directions out correctly (look for one-way streets and construction). On the map, indicate parking areas and any places where guests definitely should not park. Mention parking fees, if any. If guests may be coming from out of state, show connections to major roads and highways. Be sure to get the route names and numbers correct.

Internal Publicity

There are other methods of publicizing your event which rely on the membership of your own organization.

Chapter Mailings   The editor of the regional newsletter should be able to provide you with a mailing list of chapter presidents. Send about five copies of your event announcement to every chapter president in your region. One copy is usually enough to send to small, distant groups. Mailing event announcements to "unofficial" or "special-interest" newsletters in your own organization also works well.

Word of Mouth   Word-of-mouth advertising is free and can be one of the most effective invitations to your event. If you are not excited about your event, why should anyone else be?

Attend other events and meetings; bring event announcements and be prepared to sell tickets. If you can't attend, send an ambassador. Marjorie Carss, working on the program for an international conference to be held in her home country of Australia, took six months' study leave. She traveled all over the world, communicating with possible presenters and various professional associations, and attended other conferences covering related subjects to drum up interest.

"I made sure that chief organizers knew me as a person and they knew exactly how to contact me. I gave as clear a picture as I could convey of what their role was and how we saw their sessions being organized. I gave them information about the Australian coordinator they would be working with and those institutions where they worked. And I told them what Australia was like, what kinds of activities there were for tourists. I tried to put Australia in a context for them, and then put their sessions in a context for the whole program."

If you want to make an extra effort, you can call local organization members personally to invite them to your event. Because telephoning is time-consuming, most managers use this method only when reservations in hand are seriously under expected attendance figures. Divide up the phone list with volunteers to speed up the process.

Handbills

Handbills or flyers are used to publicize an event to the community at large, and they normally contain less information than newsletter announcements. Name, day, date, place, price, and time of event should be prominently featured. The major activity and the sponsoring organization(s) are usually mentioned.

Hints for Handsome Handbills

- Be succinct.
- Type or laser-print the greater part of the material for maximum legibility.
- Work in black and white.
- Proofread twice, then again.
- Be creative.

So keep it short and simple, and use headlines in larger type to attract attention. With very few exceptions, an event announcement should never be more than one side of a page.

Choose clear, simple typefaces rather than intricate gothic or italic styles. Don't mix too many faces; one or two is fine. For titles and emphasis, there is the option of using transfer (rub-on) lettering: Letraset, Chartpak, and others. Check a good art store. Ask to see the book put out by the manufacturer, which shows the various styles and sizes. There are also some borders you can buy. The borders come in versions that you rub on in strips or peel off and stick down like labels. (See Illustration 17, Handbill Layout, in this chapter.)

Remember that text set in all capitals is harder to read than upper and lower case. Fancy lettering and intricate borders may be attractive, but use a light touch (the notice's primary purpose is informative, not decorative).

Cut-and-Paste Method You can create good announcements with the cut-and-paste method. Check the library for old woodcuts, illuminations, and borders. Trace borders and figures from Dover Books or other graphic books free of copyright. (Respect copyright symbols on other publications; ask for permission first.) Make high-quality copies, then cut out what you need from the copies.

Be sure to paste illustrations down flat using rubber cement (it rubs off when dry, but don't rub the print off). You can eliminate shadows on the printed piece if you go around the edge of the original with white paint or Liquid Paper. Scotch Magic Transparent tape works well also (the edges don't show as much as with regular tape when reproduced).

Paper and Ribbons Don't use colored or Corrasable paper because it smudges. Don't use any ink that will run when wet. Use a fresh, dark ribbon in your printer or typewriter, especially if the printer is a dot-matrix model. When creating originals, type on only one side of a sheet of paper. It will be "backed" (printed on both sides of one sheet) at the print shop.

Copying Coin-operated photocopy machines (the kind you find in libraries) are expensive and the quality is usually poor. Visit a printer or photocopy shop for clear copies, especially when duplicating illustrations or photos. Research offset, thermography, and "stat" techniques to decide which is appropriate for your budget and your event. Don't own a laser printer and can't afford typesetting? Use clean, typed copy and photo-reduce it 10%—the result will mimic a typeset look.

Placement Distribute your flyers at least one week before the event. You should delegate as much as possible of this task because it takes a lot of time. Reasonably priced services are available for door-to-door delivery of flyers, or you may ask your volunteers to pass out handbills to each house in their neighborhood. (Note: "mailbox-stuffing" is illegal; use rubber bands to secure notices to an outside door.) You'll need at least 100 flyers for a single sweep of a medium-sized campus or shopping district.

Attaching handbills to utility poles is prohibited in some communities, so get permission beforehand. If your organization does this frequently, create a map of the community showing approved places. Give a map and a stack of flyers to each volunteer. Don't overlap assigned areas. (The map is also used after the event to remove the flyers.)

Good flyer locations are all around: store windows, hospitals, laundromats, museums, banks, transit shelters or stations, doctor's offices, building lobbies, churches, health clubs, and supermarkets. In store windows, tape two flyers back to back, so that the announcement will be visible inside and outside.

On campus, sites include all of the above, plus bulletin boards, shuttle buses, dorm halls, dining halls, museums, libraries, laundry rooms, bookstores, and next to vending machines.

Tucking notices under the wiper blades of cars can be effective for blanketing a community; do this in a shopping center on a Saturday. Don't use any notice that even faintly resembles a parking ticket in this fashion; drivers will transfer their anxiety into anger.

It's best to use staples or tape to put up your handbill; if you use pins or tacks, other people can easily remove your notice. If you do use pins or tacks, place one in each corner; even if people swipe one or two pins, your notice will still remain up.

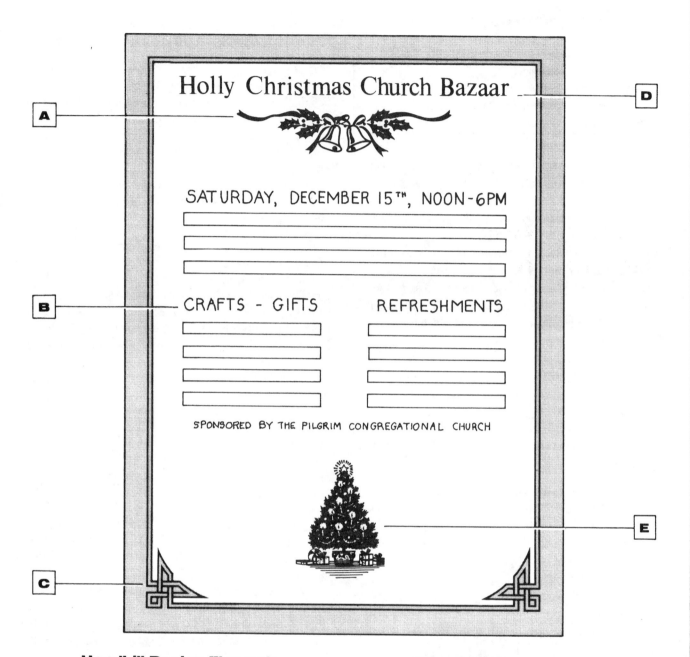

Handbill Design Elements

A Rub-on design.
B Handruled block letters or typed information.
C Rub-on border design.
D Rub-on letters.
E Original artwork.

Other Ideas:

• Ornamental rub-on initial letter.
• Cut-and-paste illustration.
• Calligraphy.
• Computer graphics.
• Vinyl stick-on letters.

Chapter 9

MEDIA RELATIONS

Public events need *public*ity. A media campaign for a special event or conference mobilizes news releases, advertising, special media, and television and radio interviews—in addition to the publicity methods described in the previous chapter.

Press Kits

First, compile and type up your mailing list. Then create your press kits. Kits are frequently assembled and packed into a "shell" (folder with pockets). Be absolutely sure to mail all of your kits on schedule.

Media Mailing List If you're lucky, your local area chamber of commerce, convention and visitors bureau, or United Way maintains a list of local media that is yours for the asking. If not, resign yourself to doing it the hard way.

The media mailing list for a small local event will be short (15-25 names); for a popular, established event in a major city, you'll need 50 names or more. The small list will contain local and/or campus newspapers, radio stations, and television stations. Include appropriate departments on campus and media directed at college employees as well as students. (If your event will be held on campus, try to obtain the sponsorship of some appropriate department: political science for a conservation group, theology for a church's refugee work, music for a theatre group's musical.) Don't forget cable television stations. The large list

should contain all of the above, plus media outside the local area.

The format of your mailing list should be columnar, with the first column headed "Names and Addresses"; the second column headed "Publishes/Deadlines" (e.g., Wednesday/due Friday); and the last column headed "Formats." (See model mailing list in this chapter.)

Look up each media outlet in the Yellow Pages under "Newspapers," "Radio Stations," and "Television Stations." At a college, ask the general switchboard; include student-run newspapers and broadcast stations. Telephone each outlet and fill in the categories on the mailing list.

Radio and TV stations usually limit a "PSA" (public service announcement) to 15, 30, or 60 seconds. Newspapers may calculate a line- or word-count limit. Stick to their guidelines, or they will ignore your notices.

When the list is typed, photocopy it and then cut off the "Names and Addresses" column to produce convenient address labels that can be taped or pasted onto envelopes for mailing.

Contents of a Press Kit
- Cover letter
- Press release
- Event fact sheet
- Organization brochure
- Graphics
- Tickets and posters (optional)

Cover Letter Always include a brief cover letter (on letterhead stationery, if possible) in which you declare the organization's nonprofit status, list any relevant connections or local organization members, and ask very politely for help in publicizing your event. Offer or enclose complimentary tickets. You can use a photocopied form letter if pressed for time, but typing a name and address on each letter is better.

Cover letters should contain phrases to catch the reader's attention. To the local college news office, you could say, "The Maintown College branch of the organization involves many alumni, students, and employees." To the town newspaper, write "Many Maintown residents will be participating in this event."

Press Release Include a typed, double-spaced "press release" (notice tailored to the media), with date, time, site, and price information underlined. A title at the top of the sheet should help to catch the reader's attention. The press release should be exactly what you would like to see or hear about your event. The announcement should be no more than three paragraphs, and should include a phone number and name to call for further information. (See the model press release in this chapter.) For radio and TV stations, clearly state "60 seconds" or "30 seconds" on the announcement. A rule of thumb is 10 seconds for every 20 words, but you should time the announcement by reading it aloud yourself.

Press Releases

- Who (name of organization, contact name and number)
- What (name and type of event)
- When (day of week, date, time)
- Where (name of site, street address)
- Why (benefit, educate, exercise, entertain)

Fact Sheet Most kits also contain an explanation and description of the event known as a "fact sheet." The fact sheet for the "Cycle Oregon" bicycle trip was a simple one-page list (see this sample fact sheet in this chapter). Some organization's fact sheets are more complicated, describing the history of the event, the organization's goals, and other information.

Brochure If your organization has a brochure, include it in the press kit. Even a newsletter or other piece can help arouse interest in your organization.

Graphics Send a clear, professional-quality black-and-white slide or print, or a good piece of artwork to those newspapers and television stations that will accept them. Don't write on the back of photos; it shows through. Photos must be action or gimmick shots; no talking heads! For television, produce a photographic slide of the event logo superimposed with an appropriate picture.

At your discretion, also include a flyer for the event, with the words "please post" in the upper right-hand corner.

Delivery Distributing these kits on time is crucial. Because of the weight of a full press kit, you may want to hand-deliver them. Mail everything at least three weeks before the media deadline. Most radio and TV stations will file your announcement in an on-the-air folder as soon as they receive it; it will be read from then until the event is over. If you are working with a particularly large mailing list, you may want to prepare all of the kits a few months before, then group them by deadlines (due two months before, due three weeks before, etc.). Just toss the envelopes into a mailbox when it's time.

All of this work should result in a respectable attendance figure for your event, and will at least educate people who don't show up. You may encourage someone to publish an article about the organization, which also fulfills your purpose in having an event open to the public. Keep in mind that many organizations coordinate media coverage on a national level, so check with your board of directors. Local publicity can usually be handled at the local level.

Advertising

If yours is a professional or hobby event, consider paid advertising in a specific trade journal or magazine. An exhibition of quilts, for example, could be advertised in *The Professional Quilter* or *Quilting*. Classified advertising lacks punch, so use small black-and-white display ads for best effect. For small local events, ads in town newspapers can be surprisingly inexpensive. Local editions of national publications, such as *TV Guide*, offer a lot of bang for the buck. Four-color advertising is normally too costly, but if donated, a four-color page can make an enormous impact.

Or, think about electrified marquees (banks and cinemas) or entrance markers (hotels, restaurants). Billboards and transit advertising are always a possibility; local advertising councils may give you free space.

18. PRESS RELEASE (MODEL)

Old Bones Society, Box 71, Chicago, IL 00077

Contact: Mr. Senior Clubman, (312) 010-1212   For Immediate Release

RESEARCH YOUR ANCESTORS THE NEWFANGLED WAY

Always wanted to know if Great-uncle Harry really was a jewel thief? A "Chip Off the Old Block" hands-on computer seminar to teach genealogical investigation will be sponsored by the Old Bones Society on Wednesday, August 23, 1989.

Ms. Technical Expert, from the Puter Consulting Company, will direct the seminar, using nine lap-top Puter computers. "Even beginners can learn the simple commands for this new database," according to Ms. Expert. "Please bring the names, birthdates, and birthplaces of any relatives you'd like to research."

This seminar will begin at 7 P.M. in the Pilgrim Room of the Suburban Library on Main Street, and run until 9 P.M. Light refreshments will be served. Advance reservations are not necessary. Admission is free. Please call Mr. Clubman at (312) 010-1212 for more information.

-End-

19. FACT SHEET (SAMPLE)

CYCLE OREGON FACT SHEET

Number of Riders: 1006

Number of States Represented: 23

Foreign Counties Represented: 3 (New Zealand, Canada, The Netherlands)

Length of Cycle Oregon Tour: 350 miles, Salem to Brookings

(Entire Route Road Swept 2 Days Prior to Kickoff)

Number of Days: 6 (Sunday, September 11 - Friday, September 16)

Number of Host Communities: 21

Number of Volunteers: Over 400

Sponsors: KGW TV 8

Nike

The Oregonian

Weyerhaeuser

Support: The Bike Gallery - Repair Van and "Sag Wagon"

Metrowest Ambulance - 3 Ambulances, 3 Paramedics, 3 EMTs

Fred Meyer - 2 Semitrucks for Riders' Personal Gear

Oregon State Patrol - 2 Escort Patrol Cars

Contact: David B. Hooper, Oregon Economic Development Dept. (503) 373-1290

Special Media (Don't Miss This Free Publicity!)

Let your local chamber of commerce know about your event; they'll help spread the word. Contact tour agencies; maybe your special event is worth an extra stop on their route.

Annual events can be published in *Chase's Annual Events*. Send a notice to Chase's Annual Events (see Resources). Convention and visitors bureaus publish calendars of special events. Many states, including Alabama, California, Idaho, Minnesota, Mississippi, Missouri, Massachusetts, Montana, Nebraska, North Carolina, Pennsylvania, South Carolina, and Texas issue quarterly calendars; some states issue annual or biannual calendars. Some publications list only essential information while others allow a paragraph or two. Send color action photos with your event information; these offices also publish and distribute glossy, general-interest brochures. The "Oregon Travel Guide," for example, includes photos from the St. Paul Rodeo, Albany Timber Carnival, Indian Salmon Feast, Sandcastle Contest at Cannon Beach, and the Pendleton Round-up. Thousands of these booklets are given to prospective tourists and convention attendees.

Arts councils and organizations also distribute special-interest booklets, such as the "Arts and Crafts Fairs List" from the Wisconsin Arts Board or the "Fairs and Festivals" pamphlet from the Tennessee Arts Commission. (These notices can also entice vendors or exhibitors to your event.)

More Printed Materials Banners or sheets can be hung in many places. Paint a large sheet with the event's name, date, and time, and place it in a prominent spot on the site. Use poles or an enlarged easel to display the banner to advantage. (Caution: slit the sheet in various spots to keep it from pulling out the posts on windy days.) Organizers of a Tudor Fair, held in connection with the Armada Exhibit at the Greenwich Maritime Museum in England, took advantage of a site problem. They draped a huge banner saying "Armada Tudor Fair, 6th-7th August" over construction scaffolding on the museum's left wing.

Use large signs on the front or back windows of your parked car to publicize the event (or, on the day of the event, to help guests locate the site). On the morning of your Saturday event, volunteers can wear sandwich boards or pass out notices in costume.

Rhonda Weiss, writing in the *Media Resource Guide*, has some creative suggestions: "Consider asking for mention in telephone books, souvenir programs for cultural or sporting events, bus benches, bus shelters, taxi panels, marquees at schools and for private or public buildings, community bulletin boards, grocery bags, milk cartons, restaurant placemats, bowling alley scoresheets, balloons, buttons, caps, even T-shirts."

Try other formats: bookmarks (distributed by local libraries and bookstores), advance discount tickets, bumper stickers, and "table tents" (folded cardboard on restaurant tables). Maybe a business sponsor would consent to using a special "postage slug" with your message printed on it.

Hotlines and Electronic Bulletin Boards

The Manhattan Chess Club runs a twenty-four-hour Chess Hotline, which spreads the word about upcoming events in the world of chess. Access to thousands of special-interest "news groups" and "bulletin boards" is available by computer. Ask your volunteers and staff if they belong to a computer network whose members would be interested in your event or organization.

Display Windows Commercial establishments sometimes own display windows that can be rented or are available free to regular customers. Libraries will frequently let local groups "piggyback" event publicity on book displays. For example, your recycling day drive display could enhance a collection of environmental books.

Plan carefully for the exhibit. It's better not to try a display at all than to do a shoddy job that makes the organization, and your event, look bad. Borrow showcase items from committee and board members. Include at least one item from each facet of the organization experience.

For example, items for the Model Railroad Club's "Travel Through Time" would include: a fully operative train on track (battery-powered); travel posters and schedules from various time periods; books on railroads and modeling; an old-fashioned lamp from a full-scale locomotive; an engineer's hat; tickets; and a handbill advertising the event.

Samples of actual items for sale can be shown to promote bazaars and auctions. Color, balance, and variety are the key factors in a display.

Media Attention

Local newspapers or radio and television stations may wish to do a story on your event. Think about the event: does it imply visual or auditory appeal? Some subjects are a natural for television, but concerts can generally be just as effective on radio. Newspapers and magazines can explain complex issues and include photos.

If you are having a performance or exhibit of some kind, make a special effort to get your local newspapers to send art reviewers. Small-town reviewers are likely to be kind, even to your amateur efforts. Volunteers will be impressed by the attention, and your organization will get more free publicity.

The managers of the Seminole Tribal Fair in Florida involve the media directly in the event. Staff member Sandy Selner thinks the system works well. "The press is invited to preview the arts and crafts the day before. We ask local artists and newspaper people to be judges. All entries are judged before the event, so the award ribbons are already on the items before the public sees them."

Find out exactly what sort of "coverage" the media want. One reporter with a pad and pencil is a very different matter from a whole camera crew. Work out mutually agreeable rules and limitations with the media *before* the event. Decide whether you, as manager, agree that the impact a larger media presence can have on your event is worth it. Check with your chapter president, too.

Tricks of the Trade   Pre-event gimmicks and setups will collar some media interest. The architect father of a Brownie in Nashville, Tennessee, constructed a replica of the city's first skyscraper out of 10,000 Girl Scout cookie crests to promote the annual cookie sale. The photo was picked up by the wire services and printed in national newspapers.

Take advantage of any connection you can make, is the philosophy of Karen Rouse, a public information director for the Massachusetts division of the American Cancer Society. For a "Great American Smokeout," the Society was able to capitalize on a famous toy: "Last year, Mr. Potato Head gave up his pipe to the Surgeon General. The Hasbro people have since stopped including the pipe in Mr. Potato Head kits. So we invited him to come on Smokeout Day . . . and the Hasbro people figured this was a good market to hit. They sent a seven-foot Mr. Potato Head. We sent him around to the radio stations, and he cut the ribbon at the Royal Sonesta Hotel [to inaugurate another smoke-free floor]. He also found his way into a number of our events at schools and hospitals."

Interviews   Cultivate any free-lance journalists that you know. Spread the word that you're hoping someone will do a story on your event. Snagging an interview spot is not easy, even in small communities. You need a "hook" to capture this kind of media attention. But special events enjoy a special advantage because if you've done your work right, the event is fresh and exciting. Choose your volunteers for interviews prudently, and actively prepare them. Bring publicity materials to any pre-event interviews and to the event.

Interview Supplies

- Fact sheet for the event
- Organization brochures (and history of the organization)
- List of officers and contacts
- Annual report
- Calendar of events and programs for the current year
- Newsletters and other publications
- Photos (for newspaper and magazine reporters)

Find out the date and time the report will appear. You will need persistence to get this information. Publicity that appears before your event will result in bigger crowds on the day of the event; unfortunately, it may be weeks after the event before your interview can be fit into the schedule. Don't expect editing privileges, even if they are promised. Many organizations complain that reports frequently feature only inaccurate quotes and poorly selected graphics. And always, four hours of filming or interviewing are condensed into two minutes or two paragraphs. It's the nature of the beast.

At the Event   Managers are usually too busy during the event to pay much attention to media representatives, so persuade someone with good public relations skills to act as spokesperson in your place. Chapter presidents and board members are usually good at this sort of thing.

When you cooperate with outside media, your job becomes even more difficult because you will be trying to please two separate audiences with conflicting needs, wants, and goals. Arrange media sessions. Provide press kits and/or a separate room, with telephones, for reporters and other media people.

Inform everyone involved before the event if you expect any television or newspaper representatives at your special event or conference. Media photographers at sporting events can pose a problem, as most want to move very close to the action to get their shot. Keep a tight leash on them and try to "set up" as much as possible to appease their desire for action shots; this may help to keep media personnel out of danger. It is difficult to protect crowds, contestants, and reporters with cameras all at the same time.

Arrange for the reporters to get as much accurate information as possible. Seat media people at different tables at banquets and seminars—they're not there to talk to each other. Introduce reporters to some sensible, long-term members. This will work out much better than if the reporters wander about and interrupt harried volunteers.

Sometimes it happens that you sent the press releases and photos, you offered free tickets, you made reminder calls, and were told that the media was not interested in your event. But then it turns out to be a dull news day, and you are suddenly "discovered" by your local television station or free-lance writer or photographer, without advance warning.

Try to remember that media attention is very important to the survival of your organization. You garner many new members and financial support from just such interactions. Don't consider occasional media contact a burden. Think of it as a device for ensuring the continuation and growth of the organization. On the other hand, evaluate carefully whether or not your event and the organization as a whole would benefit from any given media publicity before you consent to it.

Don't let stardom go to your head.

20. MEDIA MAILING LIST (MODEL)

Names & Addresses	Publishes/Deadlines	Format
Centerville Times Attn: John Journalist 888 East Street Centerville, AK 00555	daily/1 week ahead	send b&w photo
Lifestyle Editor Bigg County Herald 777 North Avenue Centerville, AK 00555	weekly/2 weeks ahead	under 50 words
"Events Around Town" Centerville Leisure 1000 Long Avenue Centerville, AK 00555	monthly/3 months ahead	send color photo
Program Director WTV Channel 99 444 West Street Centerville, AK 00555	ASAP	60 second video
WRAD Radio 222 South Road Centerville, AK 00555	ASAP	30 or 60 sec. daytime oldies

21. REGISTRATION MANAGER'S SCHEDULE

Timing	Task
5-12 months prior to event	■ Recruit and meet with committee. ■ Outline audience characteristics. ■ Determine price categories with treasurer. ■ Set deadlines for advance registration.
3-5 months prior	■ Meet monthly with both committees. ■ Draft staffing schedule. ■ Draw registration area diagram.
1-3 months prior	■ Meet monthly with both committees. ■ Attend official meetings and events to collect reservations.
1 month prior	■ Meet with both committees. ■ Join walk-through at site. ■ Make policy decisions. ■ Print up rules; distribute to crew. ■ Collate registration packets.
2 weeks prior	■ Meet with both committees.
1 week prior	■ Meet with both committees. ■ Close reservation list; type up master. ■ Coordinate table and seat allocations. ■ Give final head count to caterer. ■ Print name tags. ■ Deposit last of reservation fees.
1 day prior	■ Use checklists to organize and pack. ■ Get some sleep (well, at least try).
EVENT DAY	■ Unpack all equipment. ■ Set up registration table. ■ Open doors officially; begin registration. ■ Close registration. ■ Count money and give to treasurer.
1 day after	■ Thank all of your volunteers. ■ Make notes on event evaluation. ■ Rest and recover.
2-4 weeks after	■ Meet with committees for comment sessions. ■ Do final accounting with treasurer.

Chapter 10
REGISTRATION AND ADMISSION

"Be organized ahead of time, have the staff you're working with know what they're doing—and always smile, no matter what," are the golden rules for Julie Butler, registration whiz for the American Camping Association. "People like registration if it goes fast, if they get what they want, and if they can find what they want. . . . People love it if you look ahead down the line, recognize them, and get their packet ready for them."

Small events featuring cash only, at-the-door admission will need relatively simple arrangements and a small staff. The registration manager for large conferences, however, will have to worry about name tags, registration packets, exhibitors, and other details.

The registration area also functions as your security gate, information center, lost-and-found table, cash box, and publicity desk for upcoming events. It is generally the busiest area at the site—other than the kitchen. The registration manager is responsible for the all-important task of calculating the actual number of attendees. This figure will directly affect the table setup, the kitchen's preparation of portions, and the profit or loss figure of the event.

If your event is quite large, you may be entitled to free registration personnel from the local convention and visitors bureau. (Entitlement is usually calculated by the number of hotel beds your guests are occupying; above a certain number, fees are charged.) Consider a registration service; these businesses will handle all of your reservation, registration, and check-in, including name tags and regular bank deposits. Or purchase a personal computer software package, such as *MeetingPro*, which is supposed to track registration, print nametags and mailing labels, and produce correspondence.

Invitations

You may want to issue specific written invitations to special guests, major vendors, or ranking organization officers. The Boston Marathon, for example, invites all previous winners as well as approximately 300 world-class runners from around the world. These letters should be sent as far in advance as possible; celebrities, in particular, should be booked months in advance. If you wish to offer complimentary reservations, state so clearly in your letter. Include a self-addressed stamped envelope for reply.

Of course, some events are by invitation only. In some organizations, event volunteers send out handwritten or printed postcard invitations with their signatures to nonmember friends and acquaintances.

Reservations

Registration actually begins with the reservation process. If the person taking reservations is also the registration manager, reservations before and during the event are sure to be handled consistently. Also, the reservation list will already be familiar to the person in charge of admissions.

Advance Registration Work closely with the publicity manager. If you'll be offering many options for guests, make the registration form as simple as possible to save yourself aggravation. Always ask people to print or write clearly and leave enough space for them to do so.

Encourage as many prepaid reservations as possible. Depending on the event, your policy may be no reservations accepted after a certain date (usually one week prior to your event). This procedure benefits your cash flow—making more money available for your grocery shopping, site deposit, etc.—and prevents problems with reservations delayed in the mail.

Coordinate decisions with the facilities and finance managers, especially when handling waiting lists. Exhibitors can be particularly touchy. Julie Butler says, "The chairperson makes the decision, basically on a first-come, first-served basis, then keeps a waiting list. He also looks at the product line. Say we already signed up ten shirt people, and the first vendor on the waiting list is a shirt person, but the second vendor has a new product. He's going to give the new product a chance to be exhibited." Or perhaps you can set aside a percentage of your total booths for new vendors.

Master List   Keep a master list of all reservations and their status (paid, unpaid, companion, no banquet, etc.) as they are received. Make certain that committee and crew members have made reservations in advance (after all, they are sure attendees!). A name should accompany each reservation. Ask that group reservations list the individual names; you'll find it difficult to keep track of twelve "guests of John Doe" or seven "employees of Company X" when only three show up at a time.

Alphabetize, type up, and count this list as soon as you close reservations or one week before the event, whichever comes first. You must give a final attendance figure to your kitchen manager or caterer at some point prior to the event. Usually, you may change this figure by ten percent either way without undue hardship, but read the fine print in your catering contract.

If the size of your event makes a single reservation list too cumbersome, separate the list into alphabetical sections (A-L and M-Z or otherwise) and give a section to each registrar.

If you have access to a personal computer or word processor, computerize the reservation list. Revisions, additions, and status notations are easily updated on a computer, and multiple copies may be produced for a variety of purposes. If you are recording reservations by hand, index cards are an easy way to organize the

list. However the list is organized or whatever physical form it takes, be sure the reservations have been treated consistently.

Information Packets   The more you can tell people in advance, the better. Exchanging information before the event saves having to answer the same question over and over. Anticipate what people want to know. Many organizations send information packets or correspond with guests between the time of advance registration and the actual event dates. Some organizations send brochures; more detailed descriptions of seminars; biographies of speakers, entertainers, or presenters; map and directions for the site; and menus.

An "emergency information form" (see form in this chapter) or "liability statement" (see Chapter 12, Activities) can be filled out by participants and filed in advance.

Rules may come from the government, the site, and your organization. Make definite policies, and be prepared to enforce them, politely but firmly. Communicating these restrictions to everyone beforehand saves grief. Let people know of any special equipment they may need or if something is specifically forbidden (for example, at the recent U.S. Open Golf Tournament, coolers, radios, signs, captain's chairs, and stepladders were prohibited). Follow the example of the Music Enrichment Association; their brochure for the Oregon Coast Music Festival clearly states a policy decision: "Children welcome at the outdoor concerts. As a courtesy to performers and the audience, children under six will not be admitted to the evening performances." Hopi Indians won't let guests at events photograph, sketch, or record their dances; they also bar visitors wearing halter tops or shorts.

Brochures for exhibitors and vendors must include a map of the exhibit space (usually numbered, so that they may choose a specific booth location), booth dimensions, exhibit hours, setup and breakdown hours, and advance shipping information.

Location and Organization

Set up the registration area first, before the doors open at your site.

Your guests' first impressions of an event are formed at registration, so treat its location and organization with corresponding importance. It is important that your registration area functions efficiently; but, where it does not impede operations, do not neglect the aesthetics of the entry. The registration area is the first

22. EMERGENCY INFORMATION FORM

Name _____

Home Address _____

Company _____

Company Address _____

In case of emergency, please notify _____

Relationship to you _____

Address and Phone _____

_____

Health Insurance Company and Plan Number _____

_____

_____

Your Doctor's Name _____

Doctor's Address and Phone _____

_____

Do you have any allergies (food/drug/insect)? Specify: _____

_____

_____

Are you currently taking any prescription medicines? If so, please list _____

_____

ALL INFORMATION PROVIDED BY YOU WILL BE HELD IN ABSOLUTE CONFIDENCE. THIS FORM WILL BE DESTROYED AFTER EVENT.

point of contact with the event activities, so make it pleasant and inviting. Use tablecloths, keep supplies behind the counter, post clear information signs, and use the organization's logo as a backdrop.

The registration area is always near the principal entrance to the event. Locate the coat and luggage checkroom on the path to the registration area. It's difficult to handle cash with your arms full. Or leave enough space for guests to set down handbags, briefcases and luggage while checking in and paying for admission.

Post a copy of the reservation list. That way, guests can find their own names on the list ahead of time and speed the check-in process (if the list is numbered); second, guests can check for specific names without bothering a busy volunteer with questions about the chapter president's expected arrival.

At least one station should be devoted exclusively to the actual payment and admission process. If necessary, split the counter into a station for advance reservation check-in only and a separate station for at-the-door admissions and cash transactions. Set up another station to handle all questions. Add one more display station for membership information and publicity for upcoming events, placed away from the money and reservation station so that browsers will not cause any back-up in admitting other guests. Provide a guest book for signatures and comments about the publicity or the event itself; you might get helpful suggestions and valuable feedback.

At large meetings and conferences, registration frequently becomes backed up for hours with long lines of impatient people. The weak point is usually people with problems who slow down or stop the flow of normal registrants, particularly in a progressive arrangement where stations are sequential (the guest first stops at "registration packets," then "accommodations," "lunch tickets," and so forth in order).

This confusion *can* be eliminated! One solution is that people with problems either be taken out of the normal flow before entering (position hosts at the beginning of the line) or immediately referred out of line (to a knowledgeable "problem-solver" station). Or, have everyone form one line, but set up multiple staff (like tellers at a bank) so problem people monopolize one registrar at a time. (See Illustration 23, Registration Area, in this chapter.) In either case, establish a clear traffic pattern outlined by ropes or other barriers to maintain order. Also post large, clear signs and arrows to explain your system.

Registration Packets At conferences and meetings, you may want to pass out registration packets. Assemble and alphabetize these packets well in advance. Convention and tourist bureaus will provide brochures and maps, usually at no charge. At international conferences, ask for brochures printed in the appropriate languages. Always check information in preprinted brochures, especially if you are providing recommendations for off-site restaurants or hotels.

Packets contain a variety of information, all tucked into a "shell" (a folder with pockets):

- Name tag
- Welcome letter from site or city official
- Welcome letter from event manager
- Confirmation of accommodations
- Tourist and site leaflets
- Maps (of site and city)
- Schedules and program
- Menus (and list of nearby restaurants)
- List of participants
- Pads of paper
- Writing implements
- Evaluation forms

"Goodies" from the sponsor or the site are frequently included free of charge. Delegates to the Democratic National Convention in Atlanta received bumper stickers, mugs, balloons, pens—and red Converse sneakers.

In conjunction with special shows, one museum creates brochures, given at admission, that lead children on a treasure hunt through the exhibit, a fun *and* educational activity.

Staff

Choose experienced helpers for registration as well as novice volunteers, and rotate your staff so that one experienced person is always there. Local organization members will know and recognize other members more quickly, which speeds up the reservation process. Keep the registrars well informed, and direct questions to them. That way you, as manager, will not spend most of your time answering questions that could be handled elsewhere.

Your registrars must be friendly and courteous. Problems may arise here that require some diplomacy. All guests should be checked in, informed of the location of the coat rooms and restrooms, and welcomed to the event on behalf of the organization. Gate-crashers

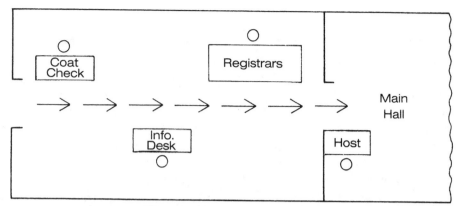

Simple Cash Admission

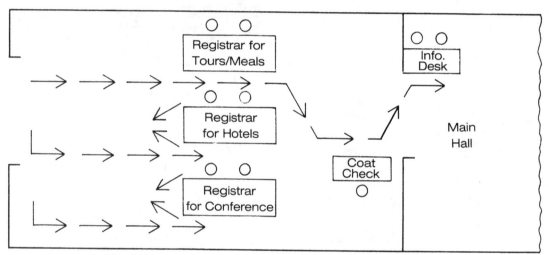

Bad Set-up for Large, Complex Registration

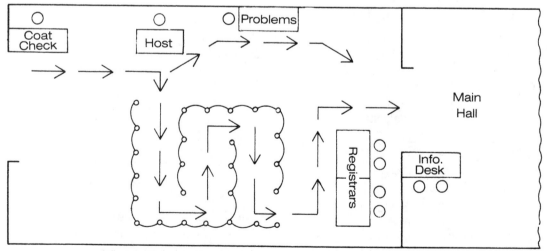

Best Set-up for Large, Complex Registration

should be dealt with firmly; registrars should see to it that they are not admitted.

In addition to being courteous, your staffers must also be reliable and trustworthy. At large, expensive events with cash admittance, the sums involved at registration can be quite tempting. Avoid problems by choosing staff scrupulously—and making frequent bank deposits.

Scheduling Arrange a rotation schedule for your staff. A busy registration table will quickly wear out the best helpers. Keep shifts to a one-hour maximum during peak times; extend them to two hours when the pace is more moderate.

Estimate the number of staff you will need as follows: assume one minute for every preregistered guest to check in with one registrar at a simple event. Double this time for complex registration, and keep adding time for "extra" parts of registration. If the registrars are also dispensing information or greeting guests at the registration table, these staff are additions to the basic estimated number needed for check-in only. Assume 80% of guests will check in prior to the main activity time. Determine peak volume; for example, your cash-admission, no-reservation, folksinging concert anticipates 300 people and the doors open one hour before the concert begins. That means 240 guests in sixty minutes, or four guests per minute. You will need a minimum of four staffers, and five would be preferable.

Closing Keep a list of no-shows and at-the-door admissions to make the final accounting easier. The event manager should receive a copy of the list, a head count, and a rough estimate of the cash flow as soon as the registration table closes. If you've fallen short of your breakeven point, you might still be able to sell leftovers or pass the hat around to make up the difference. Collect the money box as soon as registration ends and lock it in a safe place.

Policies

A policy sheet for registrars will prevent trouble. Imagine all areas of dispute and determine policies in advance. Include the following:

- Registration procedures
- Acceptable payments (MasterCard, Visa, American Express, personal check, cash only)

- Where to get more change
- How often to deposit cash
- Number of at-the-door attendees allowed
- Any items barred from event (e.g., cameras, etc.)
- How to handle lost admission tokens or tickets
- How to handle checks lost in the mail
- Age cutoff for children's or seniors' rates
- Complimentary and discount admissions
- Media representatives expected
- Speakers and entertainers expected

Admission Tokens A token of paid admittance is sometimes necessary. Some events require no proof of payment, but others use a name tag or badge, a ticket, a flower, or a program to indicate a paid reservation. It may also be necessary to differentiate categories of admission (such as no banquet, exhibit area only)—color-code your name tags. Use your judgment, but provide a mark of some kind if the hall has more than one entrance, if attendance is sizable, or if guests may come and go.

Some firms sell badges that change color overnight so you can monitor one-day guests. *Nametags Plus* is one of the software programs available that was developed to print tickets, name tags, and awards. Receipts, lists of rules, condensed schedules, or special messages from the sponsor can be printed on the reverse side of name tags or tickets.

At less formal events, consider using hand-stamps; they are an easier, more effective identification than tickets or tokens, which invariably get lost. Use the organization's logo or a calligraphic initial stamp. Stock a hypoallergenic ink pad for those who need it (don't use this special ink for everyone, as it tends to smear).

Let no one past the registration table without paying. Make no exceptions. It is too easy to lose track of people with many comings and goings. If there is a limit to the number of reservations or at-the-door attendees, stick to it. Politely turn people away if you cannot accommodate them.

Refunds Establish a refund policy. For example, anyone notifying you at least forty-eight hours ahead will have all his or her money refunded; no-shows the day of the event will not be granted refunds. Or state a simple policy: if the event loses money, no refunds are given; if the event makes money, refunds are given.

24. REGISTRATION CREW CHECKLIST

Cash register or cash box
Calculator
Change (in proportion to event size and ticket price)
Charge card machine and slips
Master registration list
Name tags, alphabetically sorted
Policy sheet
Programs
Registration packets
Tickets, hand-stamps, or admission token

Blank name tags
Blank receipts
Change-of-address forms
Liability statements

Bulletin board
Lost-and-found box
Paper
Pens and pencils
Pushpins
Ruler
Rubber bands
Scissors
Stapler
Tape

25. PROGRAM MANAGER'S SCHEDULE

Timing	Task
5-12 months prior to event	■ Recruit and meet with committee. ■ Draft tentative program theme and titles. ■ Contact possible performers and speakers.
3-5 months prior	■ Meet monthly with both committees. ■ Figure preliminary budget with treasurer. ■ Recruit judges and experts. ■ Screen and audition performers.
2-3 months prior	■ Meet monthly with both committees. ■ Draft program and schedule. ■ Select performers; negotiate contracts. ■ Sign contracts. ■ Coordinate with facilities manager. ■ Reserve backstage and dressing rooms. ■ Send program to printer.
1-2 months prior	■ Meet monthly with both committees. ■ Finish final stages of scheduling. ■ Send information packets to performers.
1 month prior	■ Meet with both committees. ■ Join walk-through at site. ■ Confirm all arrangements and contracts. ■ Rehearse speakers and entertainers. ■ Purchase prizes. ■ Print and distribute internal schedule.
1 week prior	■ Meet with both committees.
1 day prior	■ Use checklists to organize and pack. ■ Get some sleep (well, at least try).
EVENT DAY	■ Unpack all equipment. ■ Deliver speaker list to registrars' table. ■ Open event officially. ■ Check refreshments for performers. ■ Begin scheduled activities. ■ Finale for scheduled activities. ■ Pack up supplies.
1 day after	■ Thank all of your volunteers and performers. ■ Make notes on event evaluation. ■ Rest and recover.
2-4 weeks after	■ Meet with committees for comment sessions.

Chapter
PROGRAMMING CHOICES

"We had a lot of conversation about the program," remembers Dr. Judy Green, member of the program committee for a Unitarian Universalist Association continental concert. "Should the music be all hymns, since it's a concert to raise money for our hymnbook? Should it only include music by Unitarian Universalist composers? Should the texts be only Unitarian Universalist? Should every piece be accessible, the easiest kind of music, or challenging? And there was real disagreement. So we argued it out—it was actually kind of fun—and came to what I thought were good decisions."

Most special events and conferences are built around one major element: the banquet, the seminars, the concert or play, etc. More than one activity or entertainment may take place at an event and even at one time. The goal and theme of your event, as always, are the primary concerns when planning and choosing the program. Many activities can be exploited for different purposes. For example, a teacher's association might include a film *to educate* conference attendees, a library might screen a film *to entertain* during the children's hour, and a neighborhood league might show a film at the block party *to raise money*.

Principles of Program Planning

- Audition all performers.
- Avoid inappropriate entertainments or scheduling.
- Use your common sense.
- Balance fun and serious activities.
- Rehearse all speakers and entertainers.

Selection

The most important criterion for selecting the activities and entertainments for your event is suitability. Some events have traditional programs, such as Christmas pageants at Catholic schools. Include these traditional activities, but make some changes to keep the event fresh.

Plan entertainments and activities that suit the event: cheerleading chants at an alumni reunion; strolling serenaders at a Valentine's Day buffet; pie contests at a spring fair; a fire-eating magician at a Mexican carnival; sack races at a summer picnic; a spelling bee at a grade-school talent show; Christmas carols at a December dance; hay rides at a fall festival; a mystery play at a Halloween masquerade ball.

Goal Think about what kind of interactions you want among conference participants or between performers and audience. Do you want to encourage mixing and mingling? Use team sports or games and assign members randomly. Inspire competition by choosing and color-coding team clothes in advance, separating spectators by team choice, and providing trophies. Make games friendlier and more informal by choosing team members immediately before play begins, pooling spectators indiscriminately, and honoring players from each team for individual efforts.

Audience Zeren Earls tailors the roster of performers at the eleven-hour First Night in Boston, Massachusetts, for a changing audience. "The afternoon is a Children's Festival, so those performances are geared for young audiences and their families. Early evening, we schedule some storytellers. The family audience is very much kept in mind as we're scheduling." Activities later in the evening, when young, sleepy guests have gone home, are more sophisticated.

Remember your audience's needs and expectations. Icebreakers are crucial at events where strangers expect to meet and network, less important where most guests know each other. Children's attention spans are short, and so are they. Grace before a meal is mandatory in some religiously homogenous groups but unheard-of in other more diverse communities.

Many times you will be mediating the needs of more than one audience. Gene Ekenstam was involved in planning a conference for the National Association for Hospital Development. In *Fundraising Management*, he acknowledges the quandary: "If regional conferences are to be a marketplace of ideas and services, we must include consultants and vendors as fully as possible, without turning the experience into a job fair that hardly classifies it as an educational experience. Admittedly, it's a delicate balance we seek." Your vendors will always ask for more "unscheduled time" to lure participants into the exhibit area; your participants will always protest.

In the *Canadian Business Review*, V.V. Murray reveals another question of compromise: "Cultural organizations have the classic conflict between what is most popular with a mass audience and what artistic leaders think is interesting and challenging." Choose programming in tune with your organization. For example, the American Association of University Women in Lake Placid, New York, runs a book fair, and the city's garden club sponsors an annual cleanup day.

Conferences Almost all conferences and conventions have certain elements in common: opening reception (often combined with registration); keynote speech; sessions and workshops; group entertainments or tours; a theme or award banquet; and a closing speech. Other program elements are added that suit the organization and its goals. For example, the annual convention of the International Jugglers Association lasts six days and includes a welcoming party, workshops, movie night, benefit show, public show, round-the-clock open juggling, international competitions, awards banquet, annual parade, and annual business meeting.

Stephen Erickson volunteers to assemble conferences for both the National Council of University Research Administrators and the Research Administration Discussion Group. He describes the development of the sessions of one conference program this way: "To a large extent, the topics of the sessions were the result of a few meetings that the entire program committee had. We just hashed it out. What would be a good idea? What's the theme of the meeting? What will be the titles? . . . Basically, our goal was to program a set of sessions that were unusual enough to cause people to walk out talking to each other—to stir that kind of conversation."

New Member Events Many recruiting programs consist of three steps: locating and contacting prospective members, persuading them to attend an event, and follow-up procedures. Your organization may sponsor a variety of events to interest new members, such as a field visit or tour of relevant businesses or organizations; a film show or demonstration; or a seminar and discussion workshop.

Outdoor Events Two of the more popular outdoor events are sport contests and field days or picnics. The afternoon outdoor event will require a minimum amount of planning. You'll need to plan some activities, of course (see Chapter 12, Activities). Provide bathroom and changing facilities, drinking water, food (optional), and a place to sit down (preferably in the shade). Be ready with a contingency plan for bad weather (an indoor site or a rain date) and a way to find out soon enough if the weather is bad enough to require use of your contingency plan. Field day or picnic events require more time, energy, and effort than an afternoon baseball game.

Resources

Many organizations can help locate speakers for your event: American Program Bureau, International Management Group, National Speakers Club, International Platform Association, Toastmasters International, and your local convention and visitors bureau (see

Resources). For small community events, check with your chamber of commerce. Other nonprofit organizations, state library councils, and utility companies may operate their own "speakers' bureau" (a roster of available speakers); event managers in Philadelphia, Pennsylvania, for example, can choose from almost 200 speakers on tap at the electric company.

Depending on your budget and the degree of formality at your event, you may decide to hire professional entertainers or to recruit volunteers.

Volunteers The variety of free talent available is astonishing. Simply by advertising in your organization's newsletter you may acquire four clowns, six contest judges, and innumerable musicians. Likewise, professors and academic papers can be easily gathered for presentations and conferences. Just advertise early enough for deadlines to be met.

Celebrities When searching for personalities for an event (especially if you'd like them to appear for free), use the same techniques that work with financial sponsors: *match* the performer with the event, and with the specific action you'd like from them. For example, Representative Patricia Schroeder was the speaker for the opening session of the 1988 League of Women Voters Annual Convention. Tim Reid starred in the television show "Frank's Place" as the owner of a restaurant; it was natural for him to cook his special bread pudding during the "Men Who Cook" exposition in New York.

Audition Presenters Susan Jepson signs up many speakers in the course of her job at the Women's Educational and Industrial Union in Boston, Massachusetts. She advises, "Find out what their public speaking experience is. Ask them directly: 'Have you presented this before? Where have you presented it? What was the response?' If it's a borderline case, we ask for a reference."

She has a more relaxed attitude with seasoned presenters. "With experienced speakers, we describe who we expect to be the audience, the purpose of the program or the meeting, what we expect the interests and needs of the audience to be, and talk about a time frame—all the circumstances. Then we'll ask the potential presenter to develop an outline of what she could do in that time frame. . . . We know our audience, she knows her topic. We work to put the two together."

Contracts Use a contract or letter of agreement, even for volunteer performers or professionals who are donating their services. (See model correspondence in this chapter.) Don't forget to note fee schedules, number of breaks, equipment, and total number of guests (performers frequently bring companions or even whole entourages; be prepared).

The co-director of one dance performance group asks for lots of information before negotiating a price and contract. "We need to know what the event is and what the purpose of the event is. We need to know technical details. What kind of floor? What's the size of the dance space? Is there sound equipment or do we bring our own? What are the dressing room facilities? . . . Do you want a bunch of little demonstrations or an hour-long performance? Are we being asked to teach? Are we taking the whole company or just one teacher? We take into account how far we will travel to the performance. And we also take into account the affluence of the sponsor. We do feel committed to helping charitable organizations."

Get copies of speeches in advance, especially when you won't be able to rehearse the performer personally. (In desperation because of a no-show, you might present the speech yourself.) The presentation should be shaped to your audience. One participant at an international conference was distressed by the xenophobic rhetoric of a speaker who was "clearly giving a speech that he had always given to Americans before, full of references to 'beating out the Japanese'—and there were a lot of Japanese people at the conference and in the audience."

Keep up a steady correspondence with the presenter. Contracts, biographies, press releases, diagrams of performance area, schedules, sheet music, maps and directions, and other items should flow constantly back and forth.

"About a week to ten days before the program, we'll contact the speaker to remind them [of their commitment]," notes Susan Jepson, especially when the gap between the initial booking and the appearance stretches over a change of calendar year. This is also the time for a quick exchange of facts: "We let them know how big an audience we're expecting and any other new information."

Budget Consider a discount or free reservation in exchange for the services of volunteer performers. This "entertainers' discount" is common practice in some organizations but frowned upon in others. Consult

26. CORRESPONDENCE WITH PRESENTER (MODEL)

Ace Team, 2 North Ave., Smalltown, CA 00011   Phone: 555-1212

February 15, 1990

Ms. Sports Celebrity
200 Washington St.
San Diego, CA 00001

Dear Ms. Celebrity,

I'm so glad you've agreed to be the speaker for our annual athletic awards brunch. The brunch will be held on Sunday, September 16, 1990. The team is already excited. We're expecting about 150 people, mostly team members and their relatives.

We'd like you to arrive on Saturday night the 15th; we've arranged for you to stay overnight at the Holiday Inn (directions enclosed). Mary Parent, one of our volunteers, will pick you up there at 10:15 A.M., and drive you to the Smalltown high school.

There will be some opening remarks and introduction at 11 A.M. by the coach, Jane Teacher, and then the awards will be given out by you. (I'll send a list of the awards and names later.) Brunch will be served from 11:45 A.M. to 1:00 P.M. (menu to be decided, but expect healthy fruits and grains). We'll finish with the 15-minute videotape that you're bringing. The school is providing a VHS video cassette player and a television.

Mary Parent will drive you back to your hotel when the event is over, or if you prefer, she has offered to take you on a short tour of Smalltown before delivering you back to the hotel.

Again, we're really grateful. Please let us know if there is anything else you require. Thank you.

Sincerely,

John Guardian

P.S. Please send a short biography and a black-and-white photograph for publicity and program purposes. Thanks again.

with your local authorities. Certainly, professional performers who are not organization members aren't charged entrance fees, and they should be reimbursed for supplies. At a food event, they usually get a free meal; the common phraseology is, "We hope you will join us for the buffet and the rest of our event." Professionals and celebrities may be willing to donate their services; in turn, your organization should offer quality accommodations, transportation, and meals. Remember to include these costs in your budget. Performers who are members of a union will probably be more expensive, but in many cases you have no choice.

Scheduling

The scheduling of an event is one of the hardest skills for a new manager to acquire. There is a fine line to be drawn between too-tight scheduling and too-loose scheduling. A rule of thumb is to allow thirty minutes of free time per three hours of scheduled event time. Block out one hour for lunch; set a two hour limit for dinner, and a one hour limit for a cocktail "hour" (45 minutes is even better). Be absolutely certain to allow setup and breakdown time whenever necessary.

Don't make the all-too-common mistake of scheduling dawn through dinner activities at out-of-town meetings and conferences. Participants don't go to Europe to see only the inside of another convention center. Allow free time for enjoying the area as well. If you can't bear to let guests roam unsupervised, offer group tours to popular tourist spots.

Balance participatory and vicarious programs. Guests become bored if they sit through long lecture following long lecture or performer after performer, so make sure some question-and-answer sessions, coffee breaks, workshops, or other interruptions provide interest. Schedule "unscheduled" time between each major activity. Vary seated activities and activities requiring more movement; don't expect constant motion or constant stillness from your guests. Children have excessive energy and crave variety, so plan accordingly. Think about whether your guests will really enjoy, as one manager put it, "juggling eggs and agendas."

Serial Versus Overlap Serial programming is used at conferences or multi-activity events, with ten- or fifteen-minute breaks between lectures or performances. Or you can purposely overlap dual programming schedules, forcing attendees to choose which session

they'll attend. (In this case, you may prefer that ticket buyers preregister for each activity to avoid empty seminar rooms.) Stagger meeting times for best traffic flow.

Recruitment At introductory meetings to attract new members, no individual presentation should take more than thirty minutes. The entire meeting should be scheduled for less than two hours, although interested guests may be allowed to linger.

Performances Unless a performance is the major reason for the event, it should take up no more than one hour. One option is to schedule different acts of the play or sets of music performed with breaks for other activities in the intervals.

Remember that musicians, unlike taped music, need 15-25 minutes to warm up, so plan your schedule accordingly.

At large bazaars and fairs, you may want to try the "grab-bag" approach: schedule a time and set up several locations where musicians can sing, jugglers can juggle, dance music is played, and board games are set up on a convenient table. Don't schedule too many space-competing or noise-competing activities in too small an area or too short a time.

Presentations and Awards Appoint a master of ceremonies. Determine the best time to hold an official presentation and the maximum time to allow for it. Even the guest speaker at a dinner shouldn't take more than thirty minutes. At a conference, the keynote speaker should never take more than one hour, though many organizers allow ninety minutes just in case.

Generally speaking, it is not wise to hold an official presentation as the very first activity of the day because there will always be late arrivals to the event. It is equally unwise to schedule it at the end of the event, as people may leave early. Attempt to schedule presentations at a time when they will be well attended and a welcome break in the other activities.

Food Events Never schedule entertainments and presentations throughout the entire meal; the social interaction during this time is important. Don't interfere with the eating of hot food. Brief, participatory entertainments between courses, such as surprise skits or humorous award ceremonies, can be successful at certain types of events. Leave serious speeches and presentations until your guests are replete and receptive, usually after a meal. But keep these speeches short, or your guests will fall asleep.

If service is slow, start introducing honored guests during dessert. Arrange beforehand that all servers leave the room the minute the dessert and coffee have been served—clear tables *after* guests leave.

Programs Everyone involved in running the event (including all entertainers) should receive, in advance, a printed "behind-the-scenes" schedule as well as the public program.

Also, each guest should receive a public version of the program at registration. Programs can be intended as an advance publicity device, a fundraising project, a souvenir, or a written expression of gratitude. They can range from a simple admission ticket showing price, date, and event name to a glossy, stapled booklet with pictures and advertisements. Creative programs can also be placemats, memo pads, napkins, or other formats. Your budget and the nature of the event will determine the level of program you need. Decide what is essential information that attendees must carry with them, and what would be better conveyed through signs and announcements. For example, programs for plays and concerts traditionally include at least a plot synopsis and a cast and crew list. Conferences and multi-seminar offerings will need a detailed schedule and site map. Choose titles of sessions carefully; if your theme is a question, your session titles can all be answers. (See Illustration 27, Program Layout, in this chapter.)

Delays Managers should not chivvy attendees for moving too slowly (their slowness is probably an indicator of too-tight scheduling). Just make minor changes to regain momentum. Set maximum time limits for each planned activity (if the stand-up comic is getting lots of laughs at the half-hour mark, allow an extra fifteen minutes, but ask him or her to stop at the end of the forty-five minutes total that you allotted). Keep ready some back-up entertainments and activities to fill in if "dead spots" occur, the caterer is running late, or an entertainer cancels at the last minute.

Is your keynote speaker's flight running late? What if your after-dinner singer develops laryngitis the morning of the event? As Stephen Erickson, conference organizer, knows, "The worst thing you can do, obviously, is panic. The best thing you can do is remember these people are not your enemies out there . . . Just get up, after quelling your initial spurt of

panic (that has to happen), and be as laid-back as you can. Remember, the audience is on your side." His solution for a delayed speaker? Start a "problem and solution" session, inviting audience members to participate in a free-for-all discussion.

Openers and Finales

"Probably our worst idea was a parade down the main street—Highway 441. It was just too busy, there were too many logistical problems," remembers Sandy Selner, secretary for the Seminole Tribal Fair in Florida. "Now, we open the event here, on the grounds. We make a grand entry at the main gate in costume, like a circus, with flags, drums, and prayers in several languages. It really works well."

The importance of planning an opener and a finale (dance, speech, song, presentation, flaming dessert, parade, fireworks, etc.) cannot be over-emphasized. Clearly announce this selection as the first or last activity of the event.

Just as you were careful to use registration to create a positive first impression, so use the end of your event to leave the guests with a good last impression. People will start to drift away after the dance or song or toast, feeling ready to go home and having enjoyed themselves thoroughly. Allow for this "wind-down" period before starting final cleanup chores. And don't ever let cleanup signal the event's end.

Prizes

Contests have more zest when prizes are awarded, and you should budget appropriately for these. Prizes can be awarded for skill or luck. (See Chapter 12, Activities.)

For example, ask participants to fill out a ticket stub with their names and addresses; you develop a mailing list, they win a door prize.

Pick prizes to go with the theme of the contest, but don't duplicate the articles of the competition. Someone who has just won first place for "best cake" probably does not need another cake decorating kit. When the Rhode Island Advertising Club held an "Hawaiian Style" party on a cruise in their state, the raffle prize was, of course, a vacation for two in Hawaii.

Vendors, wealthier members, or local subcommittees might offer prizes and sponsor educational or informational contests for the greater benefit of the organization at large. Sponsorships are one way to involve people in your event.

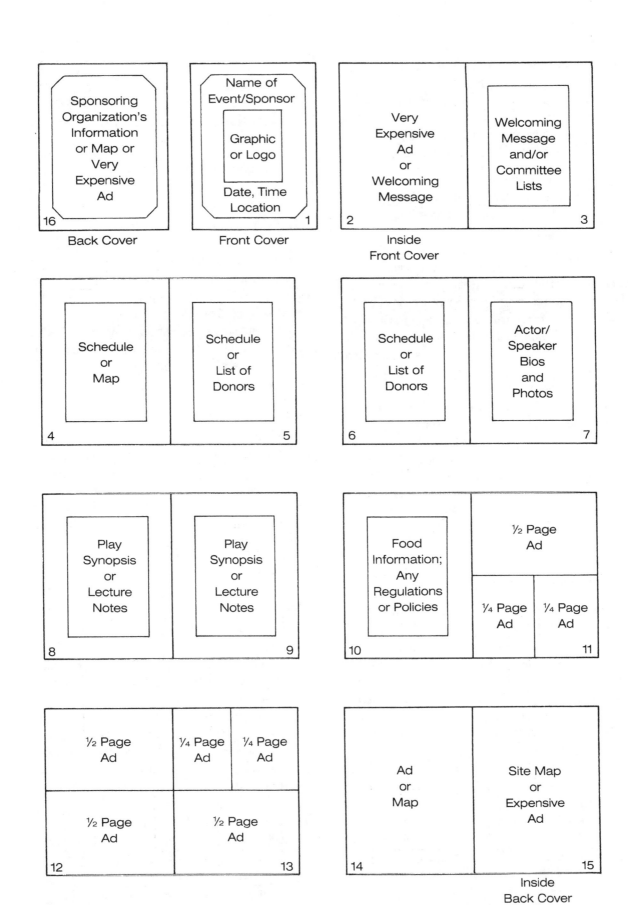

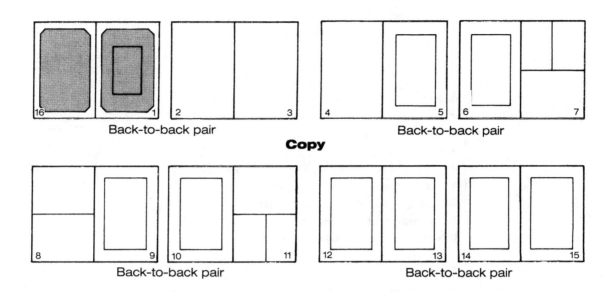

Back-to-back pair   Back-to-back pair

Copy

Back-to-back pair   Back-to-back pair

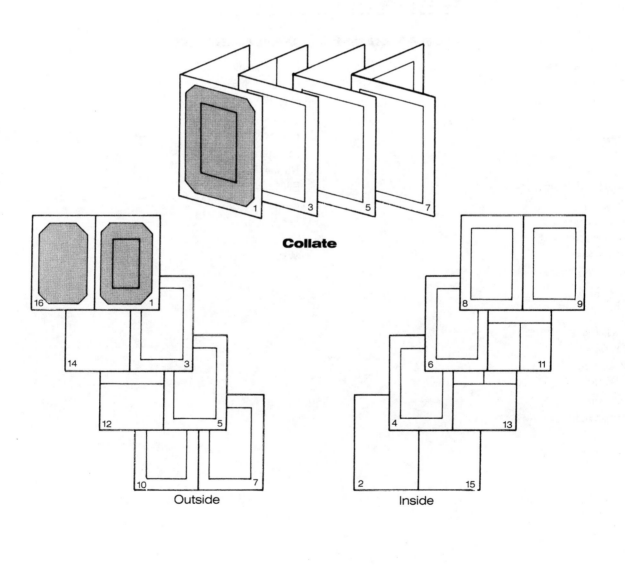

Collate

Outside   Inside

┌─ **Suggestions for Prizes** ─────────────┐

■ Appliances (televisions, computers, microwave ovens)

■ Award ribbons, plaques, or statues

■ Beverages (beer, wine, champagne)

■ Books (blank or on an appropriate subject)

■ Cars

■ Catered parties

■ Flowers, wreaths, potted plants

■ Food (usually fruit baskets or restaurant meals)

■ Gift certificates from local merchants

■ Holiday or theme items and decorations

■ Paintings, photos, or posters

■ Services or lessons (by volunteers or professionals)

■ Shopping "sprees"

■ Sport or hobby videotapes

■ Tickets (for sporting events or concerts)

■ Trips, vacations, tours

└──┘

28. PROGRAMMING CREW CHECKLIST

Audio/video cassettes
Batteries
Black electrical tape
Extension cords
Flashlight
Gels
Lights
Overhead projectors
Props
Slide projectors
Spare bulbs
Spare fuses
Tape recorder
Television
Three-prong converters

Award certificates
Prizes
Program
Schedule
Site diagrams
Speaker biographies

Blackboards
Chalk
Easels
Erasers
Paper
Pushpins
Rubber bands
Scissors
Signs
Staple gun
Transparent tape
Wide felt-tip markers

Chapter 12
ACTIVITIES

This chapter concentrates on participatory activities. Although there is some overlap with the entertainments described in the next chapter, most of the programs below are interactive in design and execution. For these activities, the event manager *coordinates* participants in group activities.

Conferences, Seminars, and Workshops

You may plan these learning activities for a local audience (aimed at nonmembers or any category of member, from neophytes to officers) or a larger national or even international audience.

"[After evaluating past sessions] we changed the structure from being just a series of presentations," says Marjorie Carss, member of the program committee for an international conference. "Supposedly there was time for discussion afterwards, but it never really occurred, of course. Speakers were mostly university people and they're used to talking to fill the time available. They really didn't allow time for discussion."

Decide ahead of time whether or not audience participation will be encouraged. Formats range from no audience participation to audience participation throughout:

- Mass lecture
- Seminar
- Panel discussion
- Practice class, clinic, or workshop
- Discussion group or "roundtable"
- One-on-one

Variations Larger conferences and conventions vary these formats. Frequently, the opening and closing sessions are called "plenary sessions," and everyone at the conference is expected to attend a mass lecture. The bulk of the conference consists of smaller seminars and workshops, usually categorized by interest or field.

Vary standard presentations with dramatic flair. One session of a National Council of University Research Administrators conference tried a novel format: to illustrate the process and give-and-take of a contract discussion, four speakers engaged in an on-stage "mock negotiation" between an imaginary corporation and university. Each "side" was given a standard contract in advance. The unscripted debate was "a good lesson," according to the session organizer. A Wesleyan Alumni Sons and Daughters Program in Connecticut included a simulated meeting of the admissions committee and mock interviews. Dialogues and debates between two or more presenters can enliven any point. A rehearsed skit or play can "juice up" even a very dry subject.

Speaker Selection Although it may seem easiest to recruit among your group, your speaker roster should reflect the scope of the event. International conferences should feature a wide variety of countries of origin, while speakers at a national conference should represent all regions of the country. Likewise, learn from Norman Mailer's experience organizing the 1986 international conference for PEN (Poets, Essayists, and Novelists): protests from women writers about the lack of female panelists drew press attention and disrupted the conference.

Exhibits Also mix in "poster sessions" or exhibits of experiments or projects. These are unstaffed, walk-in displays, usually booths with posters on the walls and sometimes relevant items on a table. The quality of these presentations can be quite uneven, since you judge ideas on paper in advance and the exhibit itself can look quite different from what was promised. However, poster sessions are well suited to certain professions; advertisers, teachers, and scientists can all take advantage of this medium.

Teleconferencing Teleconferencing—using satellite, telephone, video, and computer facilities to unite people in remote locations—is one of the newest methods of conference management.

Teleconferencing offers many benefits to large, national nonprofit corporations. Travel and hotel expenses can be virtually eliminated. A sense of togetherness among remote offices and personnel can be fostered. Many people will feel important because they can talk "directly to the top."

However, teleconferencing features some disadvantages. Because you are renting expensive, metered satellite time, scheduling for teleconferences is crucial and very detailed. Staff will sometimes mourn the loss of trips to resorts or other meeting spots. (Volunteers may have viewed these trips as vacations and a "reward" for their services.) And complaints about depersonalization may arise.

You must weigh all of these factors when considering a teleconference. Most of the experiences of planning a meeting or special event will also apply to teleconferencing. However, there are some additional problems and considerations.

You will need expert advice; contact a company that has experience in teleconferencing and be prepared to pay for it. The International Teleconferencing Association can recommend a suitable organization or consultant (see Resources). Usually, these organizations guide you through the entire process, providing staff support and technical assistance. A teleconference is

not just an ordinary conference plus pictures; it is a television show.

Pick sites and schedule as early as possible in order to reserve both satellite time and the central and remote locations. The main teleconferencing site must possess or be able to accommodate several tons of equipment. In addition to the normal staging area and audience area, the hall must be large enough for cameras, phone banks, and a control room and provide adequate power levels, good lighting, and proper acoustics.

About 15% of hotels in the United States can support teleconferencing activities, but travel time for remote participants must be considered. Since you are trying to save overnight hotel fees, choose remote facilities that are centrally located for your audience.

Although timing is more crucial in teleconferencing, the programming itself may be just like that for a non-telecast meeting or special event. Remember that satellite time is not elastic; your meeting must conform to the time structure you have been given. Don't waste expensive satellite time on a coffee break or lunch. "Be particularly careful of time zone changes, especially those which divide states," warns one teleconference organizer. "We did our first teleconference with the Southwest, and I found out just in time that El Paso, Texas, is one hour behind the rest of Texas."

Field Trips

Perhaps your wine appreciation group might enjoy a tour of a winery or brewery. Maybe your senior citizen group would appreciate seeing the paper go to press; *The Charlotte Observer* in Charlotte, North Carolina, for example, offers guided tours. Try a field trip or tour as a variation to monthly speakers at your meetings; many businesses are eager to provide free tours and product samples to large groups of prospective consumers. School buses can be rented inexpensively during vacation periods. You should be able to receive a bulk discount on admission prices.

At Vernon Downs in Vernon, New York, members of your organization can enjoy a day at the horse races. Groups of 25 or more can arrange "party plans" including parking, clubhouse admission, dinner, and a public loudspeaker message about your organization—you can even enjoy a race named after your organization and a trophy celebration.

Maybe you can wangle a special "behind-the-scenes" tour or arrange for an expert guide to accompany your group. The Victory Gardens Theater, a nonprofit group in Chicago, sponsors two annual field trips. During the Christmas holidays, members go on a theatre tour of London; in the summer, they take a shorter trip to the Shakespeare Festival in Ontario, Canada. Ask for brochures and information packages in advance of your trip so your members are better prepared for the experience.

Fundraising Events

Telethons, phone-a-thons, jail-and-bails, and many other special events were developed specifically as fundraisers. To organize a phone-a-thon, you recruit volunteers for a specific time period to telephone strangers to solicit donations. Decide in advance which of your donor groups to call, then calculate how many callers you need and how many calling sessions. Prepare a script and fact sheet for volunteer callers. Provide plenty of easy-to-fill-out pledge forms.

Jail-and-Bail   A jail-and-bail is a version of a phone-a-thon; volunteers are "jailed" for a set period of time and raise their "bail" by calling sponsors (friends and associates). Kimberly Kayser of the American Cancer Society gives a few hints about jail-and-bails: "The most important thing is the people on the committee. The success of your event depends on personal contacts, the 'pre-arrests' whom you line up ahead of time. It's in your best interests to get out the pledge materials in advance so they can raise more money. . . . Part of the marketing is that you promise this busy person they're going to spend only one hour in jail. They are picked up and brought home. All they do is give you an hour of their time to sit by the phone and collect money for you, as fast and easy as possible. Do gimmicky things: try to get the mayor in jail, or state representatives, local celebrities, TV or radio personalities, because anything like that will get you more exposure on TV or radio."

Telethons   A telethon is a televised phone-a-thon in which entertainment and appeals are broadcast and volunteers wait for strangers to call in and donate money. Put up a "morale board" to show amounts; use a thermometer or other graphic to depict progress toward the goal. Place volunteers and telephones facing this board.

Thing-a-thons   Many other versions of "-thons" have been created by special event managers to suit their organization and its members: bike-a-thons, swim-a-thons, dance-a-thons, and roller- or ice-skate-a-thons. Generally, participants pay an entry fee and enroll sponsors at a fixed rate per mile, lap, etc.

"Write-a-thons" are not fundraising events per se; these marathon letter-writing sessions are usually sponsored by political groups to send letters to political leaders and government figures.

Contests

Entrants are excited by the challenge and the chance to win prizes, *judges* are interested by the subject, and *spectators* are involved with taking sides and hoping their favorites win—remember these three "audiences" when planning contests. Winning should involve either pure skill or some combination of skill and luck.

You can tailor contests to any event. For example, as part of an open house, the University of Sydney in Australia ran a poster competition. The poster showed six students and staff from various departments of the university; entrants who correctly identified the poster people received a range of prizes.

Tips for Smooth-Running Contests

■ Set firm entry fees and deadlines.
■ Publish qualifications and sponsorship procedures.
■ Develop judging criteria.
■ Establish grounds for disqualification.

Sewing and Costume Contests   Costume, quilt, and needlework contests generate competition and accentuate talents. Consult with your local craft or costume shop for assistance and suggestions. A partial list of contest titles includes best hat, best dress or jacket in the theme colors, best embroidered tablecloth, most ornate handkerchief, best wedding headpiece. At Halloween, masquerade costume events are common; contests include best couple costume, most effective disguise, and best theme costume.

Animal Contests   Folks in Manitoba, Canada, build more than one festival around animal events, including the Boissevain Turtle Derby, the Frog Follies, the Otterburne Pig Rodeo, and the Miami Mule Days. Children are especially fond of animals, and a small side-show animal attraction at your fair or carnival can be a powerful draw for the underage set. Persuade a veterinarian or serious hobbyist to oversee this programming.

Simple all-animal shows will produce every conceivable kind of entry, so employ general prize categories such as best behaved, prettiest, oldest, youngest, best cared-for, looks most like owner, most unusual, friendliest. As famous veterinarian-turned-author James Herriot found out, it's hard to judge mixed classes of competing rabbits, dogs, and goldfish. His solution? Evaluate the young owners and award on the basis of "most knowledgeable."

Adults and teenagers may prefer to compete in horse shows. Categories include dressage, three-day eventing, stadium jumping, trick riding, roping, and obedience.

Cooking Contests Cooks are almost always looking for ways to show off their talents. Food and drink competitions attract many contestants and judges. Judgeships can be auctioned off, with fees going into prizes or towards the event. Some suggestions for these contests are best centerpiece, best decorated cake, tastiest dish (at a potluck event), food identification (blindfold taste tests), best or most imaginative breads (made into shapes and/or dyed). Consult with cooks in your organization or local gourmet and kitchenware shops for more ideas, suggestions, and possible assistance.

Games

Games can be the major activity for your event. Bingo, board games, children's games—there are numerous possibilities. Use your imagination, and always try to choose or alter the game to fit the event theme. A giant game of "Twister" might go well at some high school reunions, for example.

"Tournament-style" works well for serious adult game-players. *Always* print up the rules and distribute them in advance. Few people can be as unpleasant as someone who thinks he or she has won when the judges don't.

"Live" Board Games Life-size, real-time versions of chess, checkers, and many popular board games can be played outdoors or indoors. A raised viewing platform or balcony is indispensable for spectators and judges alike. Successful live board games require a lot of interested guests who are willing to be captive in one place for two or three hours. Sometimes this works, sometimes it doesn't.

Trivia and Word Games Riddle and pun games or contests require very little preparation—and very patient judges. Time and taste limits should be made clear in advance. Trivia contests are usually more

complicated to create, but they can be tailored specifically for the organization and/or event.

Mysteries Constructing an intriguing mystery from scratch is a fun challenge. Assemble a "cast" of players to deliver clues, question participants, and generally act as guides. These players must rehearse a few times before the day of the event so that the game will run smoothly. Or rent the cast and mystery plot. Some dramatic companies will perform interactive mysteries, but it's an expensive option.

Physical Activities and Sports

Take into account the size of your event, the number of participants, the field layout, and other factors. Although there are sure to be local favorites, some types of physical activities are popular everywhere: any team or ball sport (possibly with modified no-contact rules), dancing, golf, any category of races. Less common interests include catching greased pigs, wrestling, and martial arts combat.

Consultants Confer with the appropriate expert about the area that you choose for each activity. Delegate the handling of athletes to a volunteer (coaches or sport fans will enjoy this responsibility). Ask the weekend archer about the archery range, the dance teacher about dancing, an experienced swimmer about water polo. Try contacting the National Association of Sports Officials (see Resources). If you cannot find an expert, at least find someone who will try out the activity on the site before the event.

Refreshments Although not strictly necessary, snacks (even just cookies and lemonade) are always appreciated—and a good revenue raiser. Consider serving these refreshments throughout the event, or schedule them during an afternoon break in the contests.

Liability and Safety Many sports organizations are now so worried about liability that members must sign a general liability waiver as part of the membership application process. These are frequently called "card waivers" because they are a short statement printed on the reverse side of membership cards. In addition, anyone doing anything at an athletic event signs a separate, and usually much more complicated, waiver of liability. Always provide waivers; if necessary, print some specifically for your event. (See Liability Statement Form in this chapter.)

29. LIABILITY STATEMENT FORM

In consideration of the acceptance of my application for entry in this event, I hereby freely agree to and make the following contractual representations and agreements.

I am fully aware of the danger of participating in this event. Being a legal adult in my state of residence, and in the state where this event is to take place, and having read and understood the contents of this document, I agree and consent to the provisions contained herein.

In consideration of my being permitted to take part in this event, I agree to release, save harmless and keep indemnified the organization, its organizers and agents, officials, servants and representatives from and against all claims, actions, costs, expenses, and demands in respect to death, injury, loss or damage to my person or property, howsoever caused, arising out of or in connection with my participation in or association with this event, or travel to or return from the event, even if the same may have been contributed to or occasioned by the negligence of the said body or of any of its agents, officials, servants or representatives. It is understood and agreed that this statement is to be binding on myself, my heirs, executors, and assigns.

I grant permission to all of the aforegoing to use any photographs, motion pictures, recordings, and/or any other record of this event for any legitimate purposes.

I agree, for myself and successors, that the above representations are contractually binding, and not mere recitals, and that should I or my successors assert my claim in contravention of this agreement, I or my successors shall be liable for the expense (including legal fees) incurred by the other party or parties in defending, unless the other party or parties are finally adjudged liable on such claim for willful and wanton negligence. This agreement may not be modified orally, and a waiver of any provision shall not be construed as a modification of any other provision herein or as a consent to any other provision herein or as a consent to any subsequent waiver or modification.

Signature: _____ Date: _____

Print legal name: _____

Name and phone number of person to notify in case of emergency: _____

Event name: _____

Site name: _____

The 1988 Boston Marathon boasted 7,000 official runners and 3,000 unofficial runners, watched by about 1,000,000 spectators. The safety staff for this event included 250 Red Cross volunteers; 500 YMCA water carriers; 500 doctors, nurses, and other health professionals; and 1,200 uniformed security police. Lots of thermometers, 260 cots, 300 bags of intravenous solution, 1,000 packages of gauze and bandages, and almost 2,000 blankets were all on site for emergencies.

Insist that all entrants meet any relevant safety and experience qualifications. Advance equipment inspection will reduce potential dangers. Ask for experienced safety officers from your organization or local police auxiliary, and station them at "checkpoints" along the route. Provide identification numbers for easy spotting.

Team Sports   Team sports can be the focus of a special event. As with any game, know the rules cold and make sure your umpires and coaches are aware of any exceptions. School playing fields can usually be obtained at no cost during school vacations.

Strength and Skill   Adults and children can compete in a tug-of-war. All you need is a long, stout length of rope. A mark or stake in the ground for a boundary line works well. Puddles or mud pond boundaries add interest, excitement, and motivation. (Provide cleanup facilities.) Tug-of-war is rough on the grass because people dig in with their feet for support. So this fun activity is not advisable on manicured lawns.

Races   Cars, bicycles, horses, go-carts, wheelbarrows, feet—the list of race vehicles is limited only by your imagination. A few imaginative races on the water even specify "anything that floats" made out of strange materials and propelled by elbow grease.

Running races can be almost any distance, though ten miles or kilometers is common; witness this sampling:

- Showdown Classic, Utah - 10 kilometers
- Kickapoo Trial Trail, Illinois - 12 kilometers
- Transmountain Run, Texas - 10 miles
- Lions Run for Sight, Pennsylvania - 5 miles
- Swix Royal Gorge Cup, California - 10 kilometers

True marathons are usually longer; fundraising walk-a-thons are usually shorter.

Hoop rolling races have always been a favorite with children (use hula hoops). Foot races, sack races, three-legged races, and novelty relay races (cups of water or eggs can substitute for the traditional baton) are all perfect pursuits at relaxed picnics.

Circular race routes work best. Mark the route accurately and take spectators into account.

Archery   Archery is feasible in larger, open areas. Consult with your local archery club on requirements of space, safety regulations, and advice on setting up an archery range. Be aware of the regulations of the site; some may not think archery a safe or desirable activity.

Treasure and Scavenger Hunts   Treasure and scavenger hunts can be great fun. A good game requires lots of careful advance planning. Participants are broken into teams (usually, balanced teams work best: a child, an athlete, a new member, etc.). The list of items for scavenger and treasure hunts must be carefully prepared; they should not be too easy nor too hard to find. Timing is difficult and weather can pose a problem, so substitute alternative solutions to the puzzle if participants seem to be lagging or rain is threatening.

Dances   There are many different dances and types of music from which to choose; select music in line with your event theme. Determine in advance which dances are familiar to your guests and would be appropriate to your upcoming event. Perhaps you could ask for special dances (polkas for a Polish festival, and so forth).

Contact local dance clubs about three months beforehand; a few of their members might be willing to direct and teach dancing. Styles include square, ballroom, country, historical, or contra. Music for these dances may be familiar to your musicians, or tapes with the correct music might be available. Morris dancing and sword dancing are two "folk" practices that are fun to watch, and simple dances in these categories can be taught.

Music for dancing should be clear to the ear but not too loud. People who wish to visit and converse should be able to do so away from the dancing and music so that one activity won't interfere with the other. Be sure to provide such a space, and clearly post appropriate signs.

Musicians are not just organic tape recorders for dancing purposes, so schedule the program accordingly. Arrange for them to be served early, or set aside a special table with food for them to consume after the performance.

Other Activities Bowling on the green and bocce are not hard to learn, and sets are readily available at sports stores and toy stores. Many simpler sets are reasonably priced. Croquet, badminton, bean bags, and horseshoes are also outdoor activities that are acceptable and readily available.

Foam fights, with balls, pillows, or swords made out of foam, are harmless and very entertaining for spectators. Enliven the finals by demanding all participants balance on one foot. Activities and contests involving pets can be fun, but strict attention must be paid to health and safety; persuade at least one veterinarian to attend.

Recycling day drives can provide exercise and clean up the neighborhood at the same time. Obviously, you must provide lots of trash bags. Map out an interesting route—one that will pass by participants' homes and particularly littered parts of town. Don't expect volunteers to drag filled bags very far, and don't leave bags for a next-day municipal service (animals may rip bags open and destroy your good work overnight). A pickup truck can make the rounds every hour or so, or at the end of the day, depending on the truck's capacity.

Chapter **13**
ENTERTAINMENTS

The entertainments described in this chapter include presentations, displays, exhibitions, films, carnivals, and parades. These are all *staged* amusements for the enjoyment of a relatively passive audience.

Audiovisual and video technology can add variety and depth to special events. Even simple equipment, such as overhead transparencies and slide projectors, can enhance presentations at fundraising banquets, lectures, annual meetings, and other special events.

As manager of a special event or conference, you must decide in advance whether or not to take advantage of the available technology. Budget, purpose, expertise, and location must be evaluated in order to select media and implement planning. Integrating any equipment, from a simple background music cassette during dinner to a fully videotaped annual meeting, requires time and attention.

Rehearse, rehearse, rehearse. Ironically, the presentations will feel more alive and honest if smoothly rehearsed beforehand. If you plan an interactive question-and-answer session, practice sample questions and answers.

Recruiting New Members

You may use direct mail (see Chapter 8, Publicity) or a personal solicitation visit to persuade nonmembers to attend your event, or you may organize a free event to attract an immediate, walk-in audience. Beginning with a staged activity outdoors attracts attention and entices people inside for the other parts of the presentation.

Let people mill around for a while before calling the meeting to order. Station friendly registrars at the door to greet shy folks and write out name tags. A representative from each activity or special-interest group in your organization should bring something to demonstrate or supply literature or display items. Organization members present must wear name and title tags.

Food   Provide refreshments (mention "free munchies" in your publicity). Hot or cold nonalcoholic beverages (depending on the season) are always welcomed. Small cookies, cheese and crackers, and other finger foods are good choices. Try not to serve blatantly inappropriate foods. (See Chapter 14, Planning a Meal.)

Activities   A slide show of organization events, people, and publications is an effective "grabber." Work up a commentary; use about eighty slides for a ten-minute show. The first slide should be the logo of the organization (put this on before the meeting starts—it identifies the right room). Simple dances, crafts, discussion, or activities can happen on the spot; encourage everyone to join in.

Committee members from upcoming events, meetings, and programs should be present to discuss projects and to take names or reservations as needed. If that's not possible, hand out committee publicity. Give out brochures explaining the organization and a list of names and phone numbers of all committee contacts.

Be sure to obtain the names and phone numbers of all attendees; initiate a follow-up phone call or mailing a week or so after the new member session.

At Events Keep in mind that new members may arrive at your member-only event as guests of members or as brand-new members on their own. Arrange for each new member to be given an experienced member as a "sponsor." The sponsor introduces the new member to other members and shows him or her the ropes so the novice won't feel out of place.

Presentations and Official Business

"We do an annual awards banquet, where we thank all our volunteers and key sponsors," says Catherine Kokoski, regional coordinator for the Muscular Dystrophy Association. "Each staff person looks through his or her volunteer list and decides who will be given an award this year. There are different categories—how much this volunteer has done for the Muscular Dystrophy Association, or by the dollar amount they raised. We give out some pictures of Jerry Lewis with the poster child, calligraphed with the recipient's name. Some awards are matted and framed, some in a folder."

Nominate a master of ceremonies to coordinate and announce all official business during the event. Giving awards and prizes, welcoming guests and new members, or making special public presentations are all appropriate business. Humor in questionable taste and in-jokes (especially at large events, where some guests won't understand them) should be avoided.

Presentations and speeches require delicate handling. The national president has the right to ask for a time slot; similarly, the chapter president has the right to make a short speech. Check with them in advance; if their plans conflict with your event image and/or scheduling, discourage them tactfully and steer them in the right direction.

Performances

A visit with Santa is always a nice idea at Christmas, either as a fundraiser or just a good deed. Snapping an instant picture and giving the child a gift is traditional. Selling refreshments for parents is helpful, too.

Plays If you belong to an amateur or professional theatre group, every performance is a special event. Treat it that way, and you'll raise funds and gain new members. It's a good idea to get in touch with the International Amateur Theater Association (see Resources). Other groups can sponsor plays as part of their education or fundraising programs. A drama, comedy, variety show, musical, mime performance, recitation, or talent show can provide the focus for an event or a break during a long banquet.

Theatre parties are generally run as a fundraising effort. In this situation, you convince a professional theatre to donate (or discount) a block of tickets to your organization. Pick a play that has some significance for your group. Members of your organization purchase the tickets from you at a markup. Offer a package deal with transportation, tickets, and, of course, the party afterwards. Invite the actors, serve champagne, play classical music, and enjoy a most elegant evening.

Films and Slide Shows These media can be used during seminars as educational tools, for entertainment, or as fundraising gambits. You can borrow films from businesses and organizations (travelogues are often available from travel agencies or consulates). Some libraries circulate videotapes of classic movies or educational subjects. If you rent, remember to take advantage of your tax-exempt status. (Note: don't break any copyright or fair use laws by showing rented films and videotapes when prohibited.)

Background Music Music provided as background during an event requires careful handling. As one guest complained publicly in her local newspaper, "The band was in the corner of a large reception hall and we were seated right in front of them. It was impossible for me to converse at dinner with anyone other than the people on my immediate right and left. Bands should be more centrally located, should tone down the music during dinner when people are talking and not dancing, and should realize they are playing at a social event and not a concert." She's right: background music should not be too loud, and is not recommended at events attended by more than 100 people; it simply can't compete at that noise level.

If the site's sound system can be used, ask an expert volunteer to hook up the equipment so that music will be enhanced, both for background and for dancing. Before the meal, while people are socializing, tasteful music does provide a nice background. Select all music with an ear to appropriateness and quality. Assign someone to keep an eye on equipment and change tapes or records as needed.

Entertainers   A word-of-mouth recommendation is the best way to find entertainers such as jugglers, magicians, puppeteers, clowns, and stand-up comedians. Like caterers, these professionals will allow you to preview their work.

Agree on a performance length, as performers usually offer specific acts of different durations. Often they are willing to tailor the show or the talk to your organization and event. Clowns, for example, are not only good at children's parties; they can also be a pleasant surprise at adult events. Punch and Judy puppets entertain all age groups, and special versions of popular puppet plays can be developed for theme and traditional events. Be very careful with questions of taste in this category, especially with stand-up comedians.

Singing and Storytelling   Musicians, actors, and other talent should all be contacted through their agencies. Or use volunteers—many people can sing or tell stories, with a little encouragement or enticement. Prior notice in your event publicity will help fill your singing circle more than an announcement at the beginning of the event. Impose time limits for the convenience of all performers. Contests with prizes for best song, best poetry, or best storytelling will produce many different talents.

Sales and Auctions

There are three extra stages to events that include merchandise: collecting items and services for sale, pricing and labeling, and then displaying goods and handling transactions on the day of the event. You'll need a large, dry storage facility; a crew of persuasive collectors; a few "experts" to price and mark merchandise; and adequate transportation from storage to site. Watch out for shoplifters, and don't let your own organization members pick out the "best stuff" for themselves before the sale.

Pricing   Research prices by attending other sales. A general rule is to charge one-third to one-half of the retail price for used items, and what the market will bear for handmade goods and refreshments. Count cost of materials and labor, quality, and uniqueness. Services (gift-wrapping, housecleaning, etc.) realize the clearest profit, but administration is tricky. You *must* tag everything with a price (use "sticky-backed" labels). Solicit donations from members, from your own organization inventory, and from local businesses.

Decide whether you'll allow outside vendors. Charge these nonmembers a fee (per table or based on percentage of sales), and make sure you see a sample of their merchandise in advance. You may also organize member tables in this fashion (this saves all the collecting, pricing, and transporting work, but earns less money). Another method is a percentage-of-profits charge instead of, or in addition to, a flat table fee. Don't forget sales tax questions (see Chapter 5, Financial Management).

Flea Markets, Yard and Rummage Sales
Flea markets are very much like bazaars (discussed later in this chapter), but the sale items are the focus of the event. Don't forget to ask retail stores, police stations, dry cleaners, restaurants, hotels, and transportation businesses to donate their lost-and-found collections. Again, decide whether consignment items will be allowed.

There is usually very little else scheduled at such events to distract customers. Prepare yourself: dealers will show up hours before your opening time and try to purchase items as you unpack. Don't let them rush you—stick to your schedule. The first two hours of a yard sale will be incredibly busy; after that, business tapers off quickly.

Used items must be clean and unbroken; test all electrical appliances. Fix up merchandise for sale; remember, the labor is free and the profit direct. Segregate more valuable items, and sort what's left into "like-price" tables. Clump everything unsuitable in a "free" or "make an offer" box. Barbara Anderson, a church volunteer, notes "Clothes don't sell. They're a pain in the neck, so don't bother with them." And, she adds, "No matter what anyone says, take whatever hasn't sold and *throw it out* at the end of the sale."

Sharon Gallo, a veteran volunteer at many yard sales, emphasizes the importance of controlling the table layout of the yard sale. Augment the natural barriers of the site with physical barriers (tables, ropes, signs) to divide it into public and private areas. She touts other advantages of a continuous "counter" arrangement: it keeps buyers out of closed sections of the site; it segregates volunteers from customers; it keeps your money and change boxes isolated from the crowd; and you can restock items from your private supplies area.

Item-Specific Sales Book, bake, and plant sales are the most popular single-item sales. The profit margin on these events is usually small in proportion to the amount of volunteer effort, so don't plan them unless you can count on a continuous supply of goods (books sales at libraries, for example) or your group needs the boost of working together on this sort of project.

As with other sale events, use pretty containers for baked goods and plants. Group books by genre and package sets if possible.

Auctions Hold auctions to benefit the organization's clients, publications, retirees, or specific causes. Research and sign up business contributions (see Chapter 5, Financial Management).

Auction managers frequently forget the importance of theme. Take a lesson from David Eberhard, pastor at Trinity Lutheran Church in Detroit, Michigan. His Ugly Art Show and Auction is raising funds for building restoration. The cuisine complements the bad amateur art; hot dogs, Cheez Whiz, and Twinkies are on the menu.

And "boy auctions" (dates with popular local bachelors are sold to the highest bidder) are hot in certain philanthropic quarters.

Most event managers agree that hiring a professional auctioneer is well worth it; she or he usually makes back much more than the fee. Publicizing the beneficiaries and the items to be auctioned heightens interest. Well-written auction catalogues are critical. Draw large numbers on the back covers to use as bid numbers, or provide auction paddles. Also number each item to be auctioned. List only choice items if your catalogue space is limited. Project crisp slides of smaller items at larger auctions. Computer programs are available; the *Auction Software System* might make your record-keeping easier.

An auction in California to benefit the Incline Village/Crystal Bay Chamber of Commerce included a $100 nonrefundable auction script in the steep admission price of $300 per couple. This "auction script included" technique does raise more money but will confuse the tax-deductibility question. Often bids will be higher than the retail price. Some managers suggest posting a minimum bid to ensure fairness.

Another option is a "silent auction," where items are displayed and sealed bids are collected. At the end of the event, the envelopes are opened and the highest bidder claims the item. Of course, you save a profes-

sional auctioneer's fee, but you probably lose at least that much money because a good auctioneer excites the bidding and raises prices. Silent auctions are best deployed at a small booth in a large fair.

Timothy Duggan, a professional auctioneer, writes the *Charity Auction Newsletter*. (Free subscriptions are available; see Resources). Here are a few of his tips from that newsletter about scheduling items during your auction: "Choose popular, relatively inexpensive items for the first five items—items that everyone would like and be able to afford, e.g., a bicycle, a small screen TV, a basket of assorted liquors, a Walkman. Absolutely no services or nontangibles should be in the first five items . . . Place a showpiece item like a new car towards the middle of the sale, and place your least attractive items towards the end of the sale . . . End the sale with an inexpensive, popular item, e.g., a boombox, theater tickets."

Fairs and Exhibitions

Fairs, bazaars, and carnivals are spectacular events, generally intended for all citizens of the community. They are quite complicated events to coordinate. Your programming coordinator is your most important worker here. The theme, entertainments, decorations, and merchandise must all complement each other.

Art exhibitions, house tours, garden shows, and open houses are based on "display," so that is what you must emphasize at these events. A persuasive volunteer can convince owners to lend artwork, flowers, or even a house for the day. Good clear traffic patterns are crucial, so work out your site diagram with extra care.

A sports exhibition combines the showmanship of an exhibition with the elements of a sporting event (see Chapter 12, Activities). The Jimmy Fund, for example, has a very successful "Night of Champions" ice-skating program.

A brochure is normally given to attendees at exhibitions. Sport exhibition programs resemble concert and play programs, with an emphasis on the performers. For house tours, the brochure should include a history of the home and some of the special furnishings and features. Art show brochures are similar to auction programs and sometimes include photos of the most spectacular items.

Vendors and Exhibitors Professional craftspeople usually will not work at fairs that allow flea market items. Charges for booth prices vary from $20 for church bazaars and local festivals to ten times that for wholesale trade shows. A "juried show" (a committee selects and approves items in advance) will attract more affluent buyers. Autumn shows attract holiday shoppers, but summer shows draw browsing tourists.

Exhibitions of arts and crafts are always crowd-pleasers. At the Dauphin Ukrainian Festival in Canada, guests can watch craftspeople at work and learn how to make ethnic breads, decorate Easter eggs, and dance Ukrainian dances. (Demonstrators cannot sell booth items at the same time, so add a salesperson.)

Fairs, Bazaars, and Carnivals These "potpourri" events are really orchestrated performances. Rodeos, festivals, and other large-scale events should explode with color and transfer the audience to another place and time. For example, at an Oktoberfest, every volunteer "actor" should be dressed and behave as a German citizen; all booths should look like marketplace booths in Germany; the food should be made from authentic German recipes. Some make-believe and make-do is inevitable, but always research as thoroughly as possible to reproduce an authentic atmosphere.

Only A Booth The Boston Road Club reserved a booth at a Sports and Fitness Exposition, held on the weekend of the Boston Marathon. Club president Craig Macfarlane assembled the display. "We had a couple of bikes from our sponsors, including one of the bikes that was in the Tour de France. We had a television, showing videotapes of the Tour de France and our Club Championships. We had two or three people there giving out newsletters and applications and also answering questions. We sold T-shirts, hats, and other items."

Block Parties Block parties are a blend of recruitment events and small fairs. An initial period of hard work persuading every household on the block to join in will accomplish your "icebreaking" goal. If the long-term goal of the event is to form a neighborhood association, schedule presentations by a police crime prevention unit and recycling society during the event.

Parades Except for huge, self-sufficient parades such as Macy's annual Thanksgiving parade, parades are used in conjunction with special events, usually as an opener or finale for events with community-wide interest. As such, the parade route should be planned to involve as many streets as possible. (If children are marching, keep the parade route short, less than a mile.) Police cooperation is vital for parade organizers.

Fireworks Fireworks are quite expensive, usually $10,000 per show on up. The local fire marshal and any area airports must be notified. They will advise you of the complicated system of warning calls, sand rules, and cancellation possibilities.

30. KITCHEN MANAGER'S SCHEDULE

Timing	Task
5-12 months prior to event	■ Meet monthly with committee. ■ Outline audience characteristics. ■ Examine site and facilities. ■ Use event theme to suggest menus.
3-5 months prior	■ Figure preliminary budget with treasurer. ■ Get bids and samples from caterers. ■ Choose caterer; draft menu. ■ Negotiate and sign catering contract.
1-3 months prior	■ Meet monthly with committee and caterer. ■ Coordinate with serving manager.
1 month prior	■ Meet with caterer and committee. ■ Join walk-through at site with caterer. ■ Confirm all arrangements and contracts.
1 week prior	■ Meet with caterer and committee. ■ Confirm final head count with everyone. ■ Print and distribute menu.
1 day prior	■ Reconfirm final head count. ■ Get some sleep (well, at least try).
EVENT DAY	■ Meet with caterer and serving manager. ■ Liaison with caterer throughout event.
1 day after	■ Send thank-you letter and check to caterer. ■ Make notes for event evaluation. ■ Rest and recover.
2-4 weeks after	■ Meet with committee for comment session.

Part Five ■ Food

Chapter 14
PLANNING A MEAL

The Quaker meal, like the Quaker philosophy, concentrates on simplicity. "We do a lot of potlucks," says Elizabeth Claggett-Borne of the Society of Friends. "We post a sign-up sheet: soup, salad, bread, coordinator, and cleanup. If no one signs up, we make do with several dozen bagels and huge tubs of peanut butter. That usually inspires everyone to sign up for next week." Usually, however, meal planning is not that easy.

The two keys to a successful meal are good organization and good food. The best meals require careful planning as well as an appealing menu. Choose a reliable kitchen manager, caterer, or on-site banquet manager. Plan a tasty menu at least three months before an event to allow time for research, taste-testing, and decision-making.

Make use of available resources. You and your kitchen manager should consult your library for some cookbooks and party planning publications, and ask your friends to recommend others (see Resources). Reports from past events are another good source of information about menus. Large public and college libraries may hoard some wonderful cookbooks tucked away in the stacks; old party and menu ideas may be new to your guests.

Basic Considerations

Budget   There are four elements that exert some influence on your menu planning. First is the budget. Do not expect to serve a three-course banquet on a budget of $4 per person. Remember to include tips and taxes when applicable. Outline a sample menu and work up a budget from it (see Chapter 5, Financial Management). If the figures are not reasonable, change your menu accordingly. Be sure to start this process early. You need time to experiment with different menu combinations to find the one best suited to your budget expectations.

The Kitchen   The second element is the kitchen facility at the site. Your final menu selection must match your site. (It's tough to cook a turkey on a hot plate.) Check the site for cool storage space in addition to oven and counter space, and keep these in mind as you plan your menu.

Guests   Match your menu to your audience. You wouldn't serve pork chops at a B'nai B'rith luncheon, would you? As for sporting events: "I'm always amazed," says one volunteer, "at how much jocks can eat—and drink—after a day sweating in the sun."

In *The Complete Caterer*, Elizabeth Lawrence discusses a number of factors to consider when planning refreshments: "As you might expect, young women tend to eat more vegetables and other lighter, less fattening foods. Men of all ages eat more substantial food, young men more than anyone. . . . Younger people of both sexes consume larger quantities of nibblings, such as nachos and chips or vegetables with dips. They are also more likely to choose wine and beer over hard liquor. Older people tend to prefer less rich and more easily chewable dishes. People in their early twenties and those over 60 tend to be less adventurous in their tastes. Children are, of course, least interested in unusual food, so don't try out your anchovy surprise at a child's birthday party."

Type of Event The fourth element is the theme and atmosphere of the event. The food should reflect the nature of the event itself. For example, plan a substantial one-course lunch for picnics and field days because large amounts of simple food go over well when there are many hungry athletes present. Serve more elaborate dishes at annual meetings and fancy dress events. A softball game where everyone is dressed in T- shirt and jeans is a perfect time for an all-American barbecue; a Christmas celebration is well matched by a large banquet. Allow the event itself to "suggest" the most appropriate dining style, and be guided by the need for continuity in atmosphere.

Even if you turn over all refreshment planning to fundraising committees or professional concessions, keep an eye on their menu selections for appropriate choices. For example, an editorial in *The Animal's Agenda*, a newsletter published by the Animal Rights Network, rightly points out: "Outraged readers often send us notices of some 'animal protection' organizations' meetings and banquets that feature dead animals on the menu. They want us to expose these organizations for their hypocrisy. Indeed, it is a travesty for self-proclaimed animal defenders to be eating the objects of their concern . . . Even if the members of a group are not vegetarians, if it calls itself a 'humane society' or 'SPCA' it should—at the very least—maintain a public posture of concern for all *animals*."

Sample Menus

Here's a relatively simple menu from a church dinner in California:

Shish Kabob
Bulgur Pilaf, Rice Pilaf
Green Beans and Tomatoes
Tossed Green Salad
Lemon Oil Dressing
Baklava

And an elaborate menu from a political banquet in Washington, D.C.:

Champagne Shrimp and Scallops with
Dill Beurre Blanc
Herb Stuffed Loin of Veal with Sauce Merlot
Wild Rice
Haricots Verts
Salad of Spring Lettuce with Herbs
Demitasse and Truffles

Note that both menus include rice, salad, a meat main course, green beans, and a sweet dessert—menu planning is indeed an art as well as a science!

Caterers and Banquet Managers

You may choose to shop, cook, and serve food for your event with the help of volunteers. Some sites will insist that you choose a caterer from their short "approved" list. Most hotels and conference facilities make a banquet manager and staff part of the site package. Select a caterer from word-of-mouth recommendation or contact the National Caterers Association for advice (see Resources).

"Full-service" caterers will work on the complete meal and other aspects of the event. "No-service" or "drop-off" caterers will cook in their own facility and deliver for a charge (or you pick up). "Partial-service" caterers are least expensive and function as chefs for the day; they will prepare the meal completely at the site but usually won't do the advance shopping or menu planning.

When you are inexperienced at event management, it seems easy to lean on the experts. However, caterers know less about your organization and event than you do—but more about food. Carefully explain the theme of the event and your expectations. Let them suggest menus and share their expertise.

"One of my unsuccessful adventures with a caterer was at a conference," an event manager relates. "There was supposed to be a vegetarian lunch and a nonvegetarian lunch. Then I discovered that the caterer was doing things like putting beef stock in the vegetarian soup . . . I find that one needs to be very specific." Spell out every arrangement, every price, each detail of serving and choice of salad dressing in writing. After the banquet, it is too late to complain.

Contract Most caterer's bills will end up being about three times the cost of the food. Many caterers and event managers warn that if you change the number of guests for your event, the caterer's price will also change, sometimes dramatically. Catering contracts usually cover this problem (sometimes in small print). Don't get caught off guard! Ask in advance for three price-per-head estimates based on the minimum number of guests you're expecting; the maximum; and your best estimate. (See model contract in this chapter.)

Budget   Alice Freer, a professional events manager in Washington, D.C., explains, "The catering fee is sometimes based on hours of service. For example, three hours to set up, four hours for the event itself, then two or more hours to clean up." If your budget is tight, try to work out some cost and labor compromises, such as using your volunteers to set up tables and chairs or providing the alcohol and volunteer bartenders. Beginning caterers might donate services in exchange for free publicity and a letter of recommendation, or just for the experience.

Hotel banquet managers will demand a "guarantee" of serving numbers about two days in advance. This number will determine how many people you pay for, regardless of whether they show up and eat or not. Ask what the hotel's "overset" is (the percentage the hotel plans for above the guarantee number), then shave your guarantee number accordingly. Use good judgment; this is a tricky business.

Types of Meals

You are limited only by your budget and your imagination in choosing the type of food to serve. But "you should be realistic," according to church volunteer Sharon Gallo. "With our group, gourmet food would not be chosen because it's not feasible financially. And we have a lot of elderly members, so spicier dishes wouldn't be acceptable." Meals run the gamut from cold stand-up buffets to elaborate three- or four-course banquets.

Simple one-course meals differ from buffets primarily in that they are served rather than "help yourself." In terms of menu, there is very little distinction between them. Both are most successful when generous amounts of good food are provided.

Amounts and Timetable   A good rule of thumb for seated banquets is to plan a total of six or eight ounces of boneless meat, poultry, or fish per person, or almost two pieces of bone-in chicken per person. You'll need less for buffets.

Adapt your amounts to your circumstances. A long meal requires more food than one quickly served. A dinner that follows a full day's activities should offer more food, especially if people are unlikely to have eaten a full lunch (if your event started at 11 A.M., when do you think they ate lunch?). Serve extra snacks at midmorning and/or midafternoon if it will be a long day or a late banquet. Provide additional cool, nonalcoholic beverages if there is much physical activity or the hall is very warm.

Day-long events may require more than one meal. At casual events, ask guests to bring or buy their own lunches; you provide only the evening meal. If you provide both meals, plan a simple luncheon buffet. At weekend meetings running from Friday through Sunday, you'll find that Saturday lunch is the most well attended because it will include walk-ins and everyone has arrived by then. Overnight events necessitate breakfast in addition to lunch and supper. Again, keep it simple: continental (juice, breads, hot beverage). Consider offering brunch; this takes care of two meals at once and may allow you to get through the day providing only light refreshments between brunch and the evening banquet.

Balanced Menu   "One of the critiques we made after this year's telethon is that we want to expand, and have more health-conscious food," comments Muscular Dystrophy Association employee Catherine Kokoski. "Usually, it's all been junk food. So we want to try something different for next year, maybe fruits and yogurt. People are into health and fitness more than they used to be."

Once the basics of the menu have been decided, you and your kitchen manager should do some research into appropriate foods and their preparation. Vegetarians should be considered when planning, but strive for a balanced menu.

Given advance notice, gourmet supermarkets can procure exotic meats and fowl for you. Or, use the Yellow Pages to check the gourmet frozen food section of large grocery stores. Try using a selection of salad dressings, not just the standard vinegar and oil. Choices make the guests feel more in control—and deflect complaints.

Do not overlook simple dishes in your enthusiasm for elaborate or exotic foods. Baked ham, roast turkey, chili con carne, and pasta salad are all admirably suited to cooking for crowds. Even at fancy banquets, a few of the plainer foods are a welcome addition to the

31. CONTRACT WITH CATERER (MODEL)

NPO Caterers, 100 South St., Dallas, TX 00022   555-0000

March 16, 1990

Mr. Anxious Chairperson
Panda Protection League
10 East Street
Houston, TX 00033

Dear Mr. Chairperson,

This letter and enclosures will confirm our contract for my services at your "Panda Picnic" on Monday, September 3, 1990 (Labor Day).

The color theme is black and white. The buffet menu is attached. I'll provide all the food, ice, and beverages. And I'll bring all the necessary glassware, silverware, and plates. You will take care of setting up all tables, chairs, and tablecloths. I will arrive at noon, serve at 2 P.M., and depart by 6 P.M. I'll bring one bartender and one assistant with me; their gratuities are included in my fee.

The total cost will be $1200.00 (60 people @ $20.00 each). You must give me a final head count by Monday, August 20, 1990. The price per person will change if you have less than 55 or more than 65 guests. Any sales tax and any additional service time will be added to the final bill. Balance of payment is due by September 30, 1990. A copy of my insurance policy is enclosed. If cancellation occurs for any reason at least 7 days prior to the event, the full deposit will be refunded. If cancellation occurs for any reason within 4-7 days prior to the event, the full amount of your deposit will be forfeited. If cancellation occurs for any reason within 3 days before the event, the entire amount ($1200.00) is owed.

If this reflects your understanding, please sign below and return one copy to me along with the deposit ($600.00).

I'm looking forward to working for you on this event.

Sincerely,

Ms. Former Volunteer
NPO Caterers

Agreed _____ Date _____
   Mr. Anxious Chairperson, for Panda Protection League

menu. Custards and puddings of all kinds are inexpensive and acceptable. Sausages and other dried, spiced meats work well. Put a bowl of hard-boiled eggs on your buffet table; for the minimal preparation they take, they are a great added item. Rice, bread, and other starches are inexpensive and lend a feeling of abundance when served with each course.

Buffets   A properly arranged buffet serves the most people with the least amount of fuss.

Five Reasons to Choose Buffets

■ Small (or nonexistent) on-site kitchen
■ Shortage of tables or chairs
■ Shortage of servers
■ Small hall for activities and eating
■ Casual or picnic event

Convenience is vital in a buffet menu. Look for foods that are easy to handle. If you plan a fancy dress event, avoid heavy sauces that pose a hazard to expensive clothing. Choose simple roast meats. Serve rolls, or pre-slice large loaves of bread. Fruit, small cakes or cookies, and tarts are all good desserts for a buffet.

Abundance and variety are the keys to a tempting buffet menu. Feature several varieties of bread, an array of cheeses, and an assortment of desserts. Even within a strict budget, you can afford a few expensive or exotic items to give the illusion of extravagance.

Contrary to popular opinion, buffets are not infinitely expandable. You must know in advance roughly how many people you're feeding and plan for adequate food portions.

Banquets   Banquets require a diversified menu. Plan on one key dish (usually the meat dish) around which to structure the menu. The first course generally contains a soup or salad, and the last course the coffee or tea and desserts.

Light Refreshments   There are also many events where a complete meal is unnecessary but where some refreshments are needed. An evening of dancing and music is much enhanced by wine punch and a cold, nonalcoholic beverage plus a selection of small sweet cakes and cookies. An open market or fair is a good event at which to permit fundraising committees or enterprising individuals to sell refreshments. Check with the local authorities and the board of health for regulations about "catering" and "concessions."

When you plan refreshments to be sold to the public, remember to plan food for your volunteers. Will you create separate facilities? If so, how will you keep those facilities private? Will you give member discounts at the public food stands? If so, decide what discount will be allowed and how the members will prove their status. (And should the volunteers be forced to wait in long lines with the rest of the crowd, or will you let them "cut lines" so that they return to their job sooner?)

Potlucks   Is there really menu planning for a potluck? Yes. Successful potlucks divide cooks into categories by last names (A-J, bring main course dishes; K-R, bring side dishes; S-Z, bring desserts). The common formula is that each single person brings four servings, each couple brings eight. (The event usually supplies beverages and paper goods.)

Restaurants   Yet another option, used mostly for extremely small meetings or fairly large conferences, is a restaurant meal. One national conference of over 1,000 participants needed to provide some meal variety, as well as more intimate networking opportunities than are available at huge banquets. So, on a designated night halfway through the conference, there was no banquet, but dinner groups were arranged. As one participant described it, "You signed up on one of about a dozen lists and were given a colored sticker for your name badge. At 7 P.M., everyone flooded into the lobby of the hotel and started looking for other people with the same color tag." The "lobby scene" works as an icebreaker (guests must read other people's name tags and then they are part of a group, with a natural topic of conversation and a purpose—finding the restaurant).

Other Options   Mix and match methods to suit your purpose and budget. An organizer for a week-long conference, situated at a campus site, alternated using the campus food service for full meals and using volunteer cooks for simpler refreshments.

Selecting Beverages

Managers must decide what beverages will complement the food and the site. Some churches and other organizations will prefer no alcohol at events. A selection of both alcoholic and nonalcoholic drinks is common, but always serve at least water and one nonalcoholic beverage available in quantity as an alternative to wine or beer. In some cases, where licensing problems exist, guests bring their own alcohol; the event provides only water and nonalcoholic beverages.

Your selection of beverages will be determined by your choice of menu; choose drinks that enhance the food. Vary the selection depending on your taste, your bartender's skill, and the particular dishes you are serving.

Nonalcoholic Drinks The most common nonalcoholic beverages are soft drinks: colas and other carbonated beverages. For variety, however, try lemonade, milk, fruit juices, "mocktails" (sweet cocktails with no alcohol), milkshakes, sweet cider (hot or cold), or other specialty drinks. Supply plenty of cold drinking water, especially at the sidelines during athletic events.

Although some nonalcoholic beverages are available at the local supermarket, some drinks are better if produced in the kitchen. Freshly pressed cider can go hard if purchased too far in advance. If you must use powdered drink mix, add real fruit for extra taste (frozen strawberries make excellent, tasty ice cubes). You can make up fruit syrups ahead of time and then add water at the site.

Alcoholic Drinks Contact your liquor supplier early. No matter what type of alcohol you wish to serve, give your beverage manager the courtesy of at least one month's advance notice. This will prevent last-minute panic and ensure that your selection and prices are the best possible.

Wines are fine beverages to accompany banquets. The difficulty lies in the price; good wines in large quantity can be prohibitively expensive. If you're on a tight budget, contemplate serving hot mulled wine or cold sangria (since you're adding juice, sugar, and spices, you can use a relatively inexpensive wine). You might also get lucky and chance across a bargain case of reasonably good vintage.

Candyce Meherani, writing in *Ms.* magazine, gives an easy system for choosing wines: "Matching wine with food is more like arm wrestling than it is like checkers. That is, if you get participants of about equal strength, you can have good sport without color being the deciding factor. So, if you're eating chicken, you want a bantamweight wine, and so on . . . In general, Italian wine goes well with Italian food, French wine with French food, and so on." Always offer some white wine in addition to red.

Ask your supplier's advice when choosing ales, beers, and wines. Research price, availability, and other factors to decide on the best possible combination of beverages for your event.

Quantities A general rule for judging quantities needed is that people will drink less wine than beer, and less beer than total nonalcoholic beverages. Plan on about two alcoholic drinks per hour, per person.

Order enough ice! You'll need about two pounds of ice per three drinks (four ice cubes per drink), plus any ice cubes or blocks for coolers.

Alice Freer manages many weddings and functions in the Washington, D.C., area. Here's her table of party equivalents:

Beverage Servings

Coffee	1 pound	60 cups
Punch	1 gallon	24 people
Champagne	1 case	50 people
Liquor	1 quart	28 drinks

Containers When you make arrangements with the bartenders and supplier, come to some agreement about the serving containers. The quart or liter is the best size; it handles well for serving purposes and is readily available. The gallon jug is difficult to handle at the table and cannot be used for any sparkling alcohol. Pints are an individual serving size and will require more handling at serving time.

Beer is cheaper in kegs than in bottles. Kegs are the easiest for the bartender but the most difficult for the event manager. They are heavy, cumbersome to transport, and have a tendency to roll. Kegs are also troublesome from a server's point of view, especially at large events where the long wait for each server to fill a pitcher is not appreciated. Kegs may be a reasonable choice for an outdoor event or one where they can be set up on a table and remain stationary.

Deposits In some states, deposits are charged on bottles, cans, and kegs to ensure returns. They should be returned clean, intact, and in the proper number. Some bottles will be lost or broken, so work this cost into your budget after you agree on a price with the supplier.

Budgets Hotels and other sites that provide alcohol in the package take advantage of a large markup. "Standard" and "house" brands are the cheapest categories of alcohol. "Call" and "name" brands are more expensive, and "deluxe" and "premium" mean you'll really be paying through the nose. Ask if you can buy and bring in your own alcohol, but don't expect permission to be granted. At the least, specify exactly which brands you want and how much alcohol should be poured per drink (not "free pour").

Buy coffee by the gallon, not the cup. Never offer an "open" bar (free unlimited drinks) for the entire event. Arrange to be charged *by the opened bottle* to avoid surprise bills and nasty arguments later. You may combine a "cash" bar (guests buy all their own drinks) with an open bar to achieve a "limited" bar (anything over a certain number of drinks is paid for by the guest). Agree on a ticket system (include two drink tickets in admission packet).

Legal Issues   Alcoholic beverages are a controlled substance. In the Washington, D.C. area, for example, most caterers request that clients purchase and deliver their own liquor to the site because Washington, Maryland, and Virginia all have different laws concerning the transportation of alcohol across these state lines. To receive a cash bar permit in Utah, you must file forms and pay a fee to the state government at least a month in advance.

Many states have enacted laws that hold the providers of alcoholic beverages liable for damages caused by their intoxicated patrons. Bear this in mind when planning and serving: the intent is to provide a beverage to accompany the foods served, not to cause anyone to stagger about in alcoholic insensibility. You may wish to serve only nonalcoholic beverages for the last few hours of the event (especially an evening event) to avoid potential problems.

Minors pose another problem. Parents will not thank you if their children get drunk at your event. Whatever your responsibility is legally, you cannot afford the bad name this sort of incident gives the organization as a whole. Therefore, be aware of young people at events, and tell your servers to keep an eye on them to prevent minors from drinking any alcohol.

The minimum legal drinking age in America is currently 21. Especially at events planned to attract college students, monitoring is difficult. Many universities now insist on alcohol-free events on campus in order to avoid the issue. Less restrictive measures are also possible, such as requiring legal identification.

Desserts and Centerpieces

Decorative desserts and edible centerpieces serve two purposes: they taste good and are visually appealing. You can parade them around the hall for all to admire (especially effective for flaming desserts in darkened halls). Edible decorations are a showcase for a cook's talent. Clever table centerpieces will enhance your meal.

Baked Alaska or parfaits are simple, pretty desserts. "How about something more ambitious?" urges Jo-Ann MacElhiney, a member of the Culinary Historians of Boston. "At the coronation of Henry V's queen in 1420, they served a tiger looking into a mirror, with a man on horseback, fully armored, grasping a tiger's whelp. It is not recorded what this 'subtlety' was made of, but sugarpaste is a good guess. Sugarpaste is still used in modern cake decorating. You can get gum tragacanth (a necessary ingredient for sugarpaste) at cake decorating stores."

Ten Edible Decorations

- Treasure chest with cookie coins heaped inside (nice for fundraising campaigns)
- Bread dough animals or people (dye dough with spinach, carrot, or beet juice)
- Icing portrait of the guest of honor
- Snow (whipped cream or meringue) on chocolate tree branches
- Peacock salad (turnip body, hard-boiled egg "eyes" in leafy greens tail)
- Logo of the organization and/or the event
- Gingerbread cathedral with stained glass windows (melted Lifesavers)
- Radish roses and lettuce ferns bouquets
- Watermelon whale or Viking ship filled with fruit salad "booty"
- Just about anything that expresses the theme of the event

Managers and kitchen managers are too busy on the day of the event to be icing cookies or carving vegetables. Either make edible centerpieces and table favors in advance or let someone else do it for your event.

32. KITCHEN MANAGER'S SCHEDULE (no caterer)

Timing	Task
3-12 months prior to event	■ Recruit and meet with committee. ■ Outline audience characteristics. ■ Examine site and facilities. ■ Figure preliminary budget with treasurer. ■ Use event theme to suggest menus. ■ Draft rough menu.
1-3 months prior	■ Meet monthly with both committees. ■ Collect recipes. ■ Finish menu planning. ■ Coordinate with serving manager. ■ Prepare "tasting."
1 month prior	■ Meet with both committees. ■ Join walk-through at site. ■ Confirm all arrangements and contracts. ■ Collect items from storage.
1 week prior	■ Meet with both committees. ■ Confirm final head count with everyone. ■ Print and distribute menu. ■ Order food items. ■ Purchase nonperishable items. ■ Borrow or rent cooking equipment.
1 day prior	■ Purchase perishable foodstuffs. ■ Use checklists to organize and pack. ■ Deliver ingredients to advance cooks. ■ Transport items to the site. ■ Get some sleep (well, at least try).
EVENT DAY	■ Unpack all equipment. ■ Set up preparation areas and begin cooking. ■ Meet with serving manager. ■ Finish food preparation. ■ Clean kitchen; pack supplies.
1 day after	■ Thank all of your volunteers. ■ Clean and return all borrowed items. ■ Return nonperishables to storage. ■ Make notes for event evaluation. ■ Rest and recover.
	■ Meet with committees for comment sessions. ■ Meet with treasurer (bring receipts).

Chapter 15
FOOD PREPARATION

This chapter deals with food prepared and served at an event. Although producing the food seems to require superhuman effort, the kitchen is often everyone's favorite place to volunteer during an event. The combination of good conversation, hard work, and the challenge of quality, quantity cooking encourages teamwork, gives volunteers a sense of satisfaction, and creates edible rewards.

If the kitchen runs smoothly, if the food is properly cooked, if the meal is served on time and at the proper temperature, if the beverages are good and plentiful, there's little that can prevent a meal from being a success.

Tastings ("Try It, You'll Like It")

After you have collected your menu and recipes, prepare a "tasting." Shop for a small version of the menu and see that your cooks try out all the recipes for the food you intend to serve. This mini-meal will enable you to discover most problems before the actual meal. Do two dishes clash? Does the jelly tart recipe need to be sweeter? How much soup should be allowed per person?

If trouble is spotted, try out substitutions before the event. Find out if seasonal items will be available at the right time. Do not experiment with untried dishes—the hazards are too great.

Even if you do not hold an actual tasting, get proof in advance from your cooks that they can actually produce what they have promised. Caterers are usually willing to serve you a sample dinner or allow you to attend another of their banquets. Taste it yourself!

A tasting can also be an advance "thank-you" party for your primary helpers. The tasting is usually held about a month before the event date to give you time to change your menu or shopping plans. If the tasting is a success, then you are set to go for the actual event. Make out your shopping list and print your menu.

Shopping ("May I Ask Why You're Buying Ten Cases of Spinach?")

Before shopping for supplies, you should find out if there is an inventory of supplies for your organization. Know what is available to you and how to go about getting it. Doing this may save you money, not to mention lightening your load at the store.

Put the menu and recipes together and make a shopping list. Include cleaning supplies; pot-scrubbers, sponges, and paper towels will come in handy. Use an itemized, quantified list. Don't expect to multiply at the store; you'll make mistakes. (Bring your recipes to the store for reference.) See if the supermarket will let you order in advance; some stores will even pack and/or deliver groceries. Be specific when you order, to prevent any misunderstandings. If you need ten 6-pound chickens, say so, or you might end up with fifteen 4-pound birds.

If you cannot make advance arrangements, bring a helper and a car. It's best if the event manager and the kitchen manager make executive decisions together. Or the kitchen manager and assistants may do all the shopping without the event manager; it depends on your job descriptions.

Shop systematically, and bring a calculator. Double-check your list; it's easy to forget items. Try not to be unnerved when people stare as you select 30 chickens, 65 loaves of bread, 12 cases of canned peaches, and 20 pounds of vegetables.

Where to Shop Buy at large markets, co-ops, or wholesale discount places whenever possible. To save time and energy, shop at twenty-four-hour warehouse stores during quiet hours. Don't purchase perishables (bread, meat, fresh produce, milk) more than a few days in advance. Look for sales. Always ask about discounts when buying large quantities. Buy cheaper generic goods, especially paper and plastic products (but be sure these are heavy-duty). Pick up fruit and vegetables at open-air markets. Shop wholesalers for large quantities of meat, fowl, or fish.

Quantity Cooking

Recipes do not always enlarge easily. It is simple to cook a dish that you must "stir constantly until boiling" when you're making a single quart and it boils in four minutes. But five gallons may take almost an hour to boil; do you really want to stir it all that time? Scrambled eggs for a PTA brunch might mean scheduling a half-hour for egg-cracking.

Watch your cooking schedules; cooking in large quantities automatically means a longer cooking time. The hot dish for the first course and the hot dish for the third course probably cannot be cooked on the same burner because of the length of time it takes to heat a large pot. You may also need slightly higher oven temperatures.

Concentrates Soups and beverages can often be made in advance with about one-quarter the amount of water or broth needed. Transport cooled, concentrated liquids to the site in gallon bottles. Put soup in a large pot, add water, then heat and serve. Transfer beverage syrup to pitchers, add water, then chill and serve.

Time-savers The more short cuts, the better. Frozen pie crusts can save lots of time and tempers, and you get a cooking and serving container that you don't need to wash. Commercial butter pats, frozen

vegetables, and pre-sliced meats all save time and energy when cooking in bulk.

Equipment Ovens in industrial kitchens are usually slower to preheat than residential ovens. Dishwashers in industrial kitchens should be operated by site staff.

Organization

Many dishes can be prepared in advance and reheated at the site. With advance notice, good cooks may be trusted to cook at home. You may want to ask them to pick up their own ingredients and be reimbursed later (agree on the approximate cost beforehand). Ascertain in advance that they own adequate equipment, stove, and refrigeration. Also work out how and when food will be transported to the site.

When you get home from shopping, divide the groceries into piles to be distributed to advance cooks. Provide these volunteers with everything necessary in separate bags: include spices, detailed instructions, and your phone number. (Double-check supplies with recipes.) Offer pickup and delivery if possible.

After organizing items for advance cooks, divide up bulk items, then organize all the other ingredients and measure, bag, and label them (according to what dish they belong to). Refrigerate perishables. Pack nonperishables and specific equipment or special utensils together and clearly mark the bags. List perishables that are being refrigerated so you can match them with nonperishables. Put strips of colored tape on personal and organization equipment for instant identification. Pack cleaning supplies together. The more organized you are now, the easier it will be to delegate tasks at the site.

On the Day of the Event

Here's how the schedule looks for one church's Sunday meal:

Saturday—precook and prepare as much as possible; season meat, peel potatoes, set table

Sunday 6:30 A.M.—minister starts ovens; later, moves meat pans from refrigerator to ovens

9:30 A.M.—turn on pot of potato water

10:30 A.M.—begin cooking vegetables

11 A.M.—volunteers leave service early, final cooking and table-setting

11:30 A.M.—service ends; grace; meal begins

1 P.M.—meal ends; cleanup begins

2 P.M.—cleanup ends

Set up the Kitchen When you arrive at the site on the day of the event, keep the kitchen isolated for the first half-hour or so while you unpack and get everything in place. Don't let any more people than necessary into the kitchen at one time. Post the menu and cooking schedules. Set up the serving passageways. If possible, use a cool side room for cold dishes; this system frees up kitchen space. Fasten trash bags to the edge of the counters with duct tape so that workers can clean as they cook.

Posting lists is an excellent way of organizing your kitchen. It frees you from repeating instructions and lessens the chance of items being forgotten or mixed up. Make up these lists in advance. Put all ingredients for each dish at a particular countertop, with name of dish, person responsible for cooking, ingredients, equipment, recipe, special instructions, estimated cooking time, what time dish should be heated, and a list of what's in the refrigerator that goes into the dish. The perishable ingredients go in a clearly labeled bag in the refrigerator (i.e., "eggs and cream for mousse dessert"). Or, try an assembly line method for dishes with several independent steps.

The kitchen manager should not cook every dish, but should check on the progress of the individual cooks regularly. Delegate tasks. Don't waste a good cook washing spinach—suit the person to the task. You can turn non-cooks into dishwashers or coach them to perform simple cooking tasks. Give a quick demonstration and check back later to see how the volunteer is doing.

Cleanup As much as you can, clean as you go. This is particularly important in a multi-course meal and when the same serving dishes will be required later in the meal. Soak messy pots as soon as possible. Bring really messy pans home in a trash bag to soak and deal with later (if they belong to you or your group rather than to the site).

Once the food has been cooked and served, the kitchen manager should leave the kitchen. The job is done, and like the rest of the workforce, the kitchen manager deserves a chance to socialize and enjoy the evening. Call in the cleanup crew to handle the dirty kitchen and pots and pans. Thank the kitchen crew profusely.

Emergencies ("I Thought That Was Salt, Not Sugar!")

Occasionally, something goes wrong. You should remain calm and reassuring. Decide how to correct the situation. If a dish is ruined or burned, *do not* serve it. That scorched soup or uncooked chicken will be the dish that everyone remembers afterward. Prepare more starch and vegetables. Send someone to the store for more cheese, fruit, or bread. Buy a precooked ham or turkey breast that you can just heat and slice, or send out to the deli for cold sliced meats.

Here are a few easily obtainable items you could purchase to round out a skimpy meal without a great outlay of cash:

- Breads and spreads (honey, butter, strawberry preserves, orange marmalade)
- Frozen vegetables (buy carrots, peas, or spinach; heat up and toss with butter or vinegar and herbs)
- Quick rice
- Fresh vegetables (cut up carrots, cauliflower, and broccoli, or serve shredded cabbage tossed with oil and vinegar)
- Fresh fruit: apples, oranges, pears
- Thin gingersnap cookies, with bowls of sweetened whipped cream or applesauce
- Sliced deli meats (ham, salami, turkey) rolled into tubes or cones.

Health

Salmonella and food poisoning are real dangers at special events. Be sure that all food is adequately refrigerated before serving. Don't let any food sit out for more than a couple of hours. This is especially applicable to buffets and outdoor events. Dishes cooked with milk often acquire a bad taste if left overnight, even in the refrigerator. Plan to cook these on the day of the event, if possible.

Since many garbage bags are chemically treated, don't use garbage bags for food storage unless food is wrapped tightly in some other container first. Improvise cool storage by borrowing coolers or by filling plastic-lined boxes with ice. A cold porch or hall can be used for refrigeration, provided food is secure from vermin and not too cold (some foods don't freeze well). See that a first-aid kit is available.

33. KITCHEN CREW CHECKLIST

Aprons
Can openers
Corkscrews/bottle openers
Dishtowels
Knives
Ladles
Matches
Pots and pans
Potholders
Scissors
Spatulas
Stirring
Spoons
Strainers

Calculator
Cookbooks
Lists
Menus
Paper
Pens
Schedule

Aluminum foil
Dishwashing liquid
Duct tape
Hand soap
Paper towels
Steel wool
Trash bags
Ziplock bags

34. SERVING MANAGER'S SCHEDULE

Timing	Task
5-12 months prior to event	■ Recruit and meet with committee. ■ Examine site and facilities. ■ Coordinate with kitchen manager. ■ Use event theme to suggest serving method.
3-5 months prior	■ Meet monthly with both committees. ■ Figure preliminary budget with treasurer. ■ Draft rough table diagrams.
1-3 months prior	■ Meet monthly with both committees. ■ Coordinate with decorating committee. ■ Attend "tasting."
1 month prior	■ Meet with both committees. ■ Join walk-through at site. ■ Confirm all arrangements and contracts. ■ Collect items from storage.
1 week prior	■ Meet with both committees. ■ Confirm final head count with everyone. ■ Draw final table diagrams; distribute. ■ Distribute menu to serving crew. ■ Borrow or rent serving equipment.
1 day prior	■ Use checklists to organize and pack. ■ Transport items to the site. ■ Get some sleep (well, at least try).
EVENT DAY	■ Unpack all equipment. ■ Set up serving stations. ■ Meet with kitchen manager. ■ Meet with serving crew. ■ Use preset to test servers. ■ Serve meal. ■ Clean kitchen; pack supplies.
1 day after	■ Thank all of your volunteers. ■ Clean and return all borrowed items. ■ Return nonperishables to storage. ■ Make notes for event evaluation. ■ Rest and recover.
2-4 weeks after	■ Meet with committees for comment sessions.

Chapter 16
SERVING AND CLEANING

"Develop an eye for pleasing presentation," advises Alicia Rodriguez, president of Meeting Management Resources, a consulting and seminar business in Wellesley, Massachusetts. "When you sit down to a meal, someone has thought about the colors on your plate, the nutritional value of your meal, and the way the table linens coordinate with the walls and ceiling."

Serving Styles

Just as you can choose from several types of meals, so you can select from several types of parallel meal service. Eight styles are listed below, ranked roughly according to degree of difficulty (i.e., how many servers you will need per person) and therefore in order of informal to formal.

Mixing styles during one meal to suit meal phases can make good sense. For example, you may begin with guests standing and appetizers passed on trays by servers, then move into the banquet room, where preset salad, rolls, and butter wait on each table. The soup follows, served French, then silver service main course. Back on your feet to end with a dessert buffet. Or, use salad and beverage buffet stations to simplify family-style serving.

At informal events without dinner presentations, stagger the eating hours to avert crowding and delays.

Serving Styles*

- Buffet: food tables, guests stand and serve themselves
- Reception: food passed on trays by servers, guests stand and serve themselves
- Action station: food is prepared by server at buffet stations, guests stand and serve themselves
- Cafeteria style: guests stand in line and are served; take their plates back to table to sit
- Family style: seated, guests serve themselves from common dishes on the table
- Preset: food is already on the table when guests seat themselves
- Russian or silver service: food is served to guests from serving platters while they are seated
- French service: food is brought to the table on a *gueridon* (cart with wheels) to *rechauder* (reheat), sauté, or flambé, then served to guests while they are seated

*Some of these terms courtesy of Diane Prescott of the Hyatt Regency Hotel.

R. David Smith, manager of special events at the Nature Conservancy in Arlington, Virginia, shared this hint with *Meeting Manager* readers: "Instead of serving hors d'oeuvres buffet-style at a cocktail reception, hire white-gloved waiters to pass the food on silver trays. You'll save on food costs (people eat three to four pieces with this method compared to seven or eight pieces when served buffet-style); you'll save on flowers that would normally decorate a buffet table; and people don't have to stop their conversations to go to the buffet table. Also, you can serve fancier food because you're serving less of it."

Diagram the Serving Area Work with the facilities manager in advance on table diagrams and setups (see Chapter 7, Facilities). An aisle at least four feet wide between tables will allow servers and guests to move comfortably between tables. Minimize the number of guests who will be seated with their backs to the head table. No one should be seated behind the speaker podium. Everyone at the head table sits on one side of the table facing the rest of the hall. Consider arranging a space in front of the head table so that entertainments may be staged from this central location. On the day of the event, make sure that the table chart has been successfully translated into the actual table setup.

Number or name tables on your charts. Coordinate table assignments with the registration manager. Table hosts can be designated to select and introduce guests for each table. You may let guests reserve specific tables in advance or assign spaces by the date the reservation is received. Two-way place cards enable everyone at a table to learn names. At large events with no preregistration, you can post a sign-up sheet for tables to avoid the crowding and rush of a "first-come, first-served" seating system. Or use a host at the dining room entrance to assign tables.

In *Fundraising Management*, Del Frnka counsels, "All parties should look full to the point of oversubscription. Nothing is more dismal than empty places at a seated dinner. Although it requires a great deal more effort, it is well worth the trouble to pull tables from the dining room in order to eliminate 'guest gaps.' "

Appearances Presentation affects the look, color, taste, and texture of food. Coordinate serving and personal dishes, table linens and decorations, and garnishes to achieve the best effect. Candlelight always helps the appearance of food. Choose table decorations that are ten inches or less in height so as not to disturb conversation; small votive candles work well.

"There's no excuse for a boring banquet," asserts Jo-Ann MacElhiney, member of the Culinary Historians of Boston. "Garnishes can do a lot for the appearance of food. Ring a plate of sliced meats with parsley sprigs, carve crowns from orange shells, add a scallion brush or a carrot curl here and there, and the whole

meal will seem transformed. These minimal extra efforts really pay off."

Bartending Serve ice water throughout your event. Recruit volunteers to open bottles or pour drinks. It's a nice touch to use aprons featuring the insignia of the organization. Provide extra openers and corkscrews (bright colored ribbons or tape will help you keep track of them). Extra-absorbent towels will come in handy, too. If there is a deposit system in your state, rinse empty bottles before returning them to the store.

The Serving Manager The serving manager, known as a "captain" in restaurants and hotels, supervises the serving of a meal and is the liaison between the kitchen manager and the guests. One of the catering assistants will assume this role during catered functions. Even with cafeteria or buffet-style service, use a "host" to assign tables and oversee service.

If the captain is a good one, the food will be served neatly, on schedule, and with little commotion. Efficiency is the name of the game. The organization is done behind the scenes, but when done correctly, all servers will know exactly which tables they are responsible for, what is being served when, and how many portions are allotted per table. The ideal to shoot for, even at large events, is that all plates will be "dropped" (placed on the table) within a ten-minute span.

The captain must constantly be aware of numbers: how much "yield" per dish (number of pieces or servings per order), how many reservations, how many tables, how many people at each table.

Serving Staff The best ratio of volunteer servers to seated guests is two servers per table of eight to ten people. Servers' duties include serving food, pouring beverages, collecting used plates, and running errands for the captain. Therefore, a full-service seated dinner for 100 people will require about 20 volunteer servers in order to be adequately served. Sometimes, not enough servers will volunteer. An alternative to formal serving is to use volunteers from each table. This works reasonably well for small, informal events. If you hire professional servers or the site provides staff, you need only half as many servers (e.g., one server per table, or 10 servers per 100 seated guests).

Lower the number of servers for less complicated serving styles, and raise it for more complicated serving styles. For a standing reception of 100 people, you'll need a professional staff of seven: two bartenders, four servers, and one captain. (One knowledgeable bartender can serve 50 to 75 people adequately.)

Serving Procedures

Post a table chart and menu at the point where food passes from the kitchen to the servers. The captain is stationed at this passthrough point throughout the meal, unless problems crop up in the dining room.

Meeting The captain should schedule a brief discussion of the menu, portions, and ingredients with the kitchen manager about an hour prior to the food's being served to be sure of last-minute changes. Immediately after this meeting, the captain should assemble the serving crew. The captain will then reiterate the table placement, show the diagram, assign servers to specific tables, and review the menu.

Preset Preset materials should also be distributed at this time. A standard preset is water, bread, butter, and salt and pepper. (Salt and pepper can be served in tiny paper candy cups.) The preset is the preliminary test of servers. The captain can check at this point to see that each table is properly preset before the meal actually begins.

Head Table

Event managers choose whether or not to plan a head table, and the choice is usually determined by the type of food planned. A simple one-course affair can easily do without a head table. A large banquet or any menu with a formal setting probably demands a head table.

Guests Invitations to sit at the head table are most properly extended by the ranking local officer, usually the chapter president. That individual will also know the politics involved in choosing those for seating at the head table. Invitations are only extended to those who are expected to attend.

Those seated at the head table include national officers, guests of honor, featured speakers, and other notables—and don't forget the companions of invited guests. Any remaining places are filled as the chapter president wishes with the winners of awards, organization members returning after long absences, the manager of the previous event, you yourself, or whoever the president recommends.

Buffets

"I don't like lines," declares Alice Freer, owner of Alice Freer Special Events in Washington, D.C. "So I've learned a lot of logistic things to do so that won't happen. One way is to use what we call 'stations'—several buffets around, all with different items. Also, this arrangement works as an icebreaker with the guests. They ask each other about items at the other stations."

Locations Will you be serving everything at once? If so, you will need more table space than if you serve the food in courses. Review the size of the hall and the layout of the site. It might be possible to set up one long row of tables with a line of guests passing on each side. You could also start a line at each end of one long table, working towards the center. Or start the line from the center of the table, moving both left and right. Duplicate tables at each end of the hall can cut down on a mob scene; provide duplicates of each serving dish. Allow enough space for the line and easy access to and from the tables for both the guests and the helpers refilling empty serving dishes.

Beware, even the best-laid plans can come to naught. One event manager remembers this incident at a school in Wisconsin: "We had a really elaborate table display, done by a volunteer who was a professional interior decorator. The room didn't look anything like the school cafeteria. It was just gorgeous. The buffet lines were supposed to go on the outside of this display. Well, the guests didn't want to do it that way. They wanted to go on both sides, so they just moved all the tables. The display did not fall over, luckily, but it looked utterly ridiculous because all those carefully formed displays were scattered. The reception line was moving slowly, so maybe they were hungry. The next year, we set it up with huge plants at the corners—made it bigger and heavier so it couldn't be adjusted. The guests moved the plants. They did exactly the same thing again. I couldn't believe it." This is a prime example of why an event manager needs a good sense of humor!

Table Designs Professional caterers and hotel banquet managers try to place food on buffets at different levels to heighten interest. Make sure your table elevations are well built and sturdy; use weighted boxes if necessary. Marian Walke, a seasoned event manager and cook, volunteers for the Society for Creative Anachronism. She developed an inexpensive freestanding tiered buffet layout. The buffet tables are arranged so that they can be approached from all four sides, and duplicate servings are placed on each side. Each table is constructed in three tiers so that food can be placed at various levels. Here's how it's done:

1. Unfold four standard rectangular tables and set up as shown, inner corners touching.

2. Cover these first tables with overlapped lengths of linen or paper. Stack two to four more standard tables (rectangular or round), with legs folded up, in the center to form a second tier. Put wedges in to steady the stacked tables where necessary.

3. Cover the stacked tables very neatly with linen or paper tablecloths (use hospital corners, if possible), and top with several hard plastic bakery carrying trays or large plastic milk cartons, upside down.

4. Cover these trays or cartons with more tablecloths. Place an edible centerpiece and/or a large-size menu on the highest tier.

Presto! You have a space-efficient, functional, and very attractive buffet setup. (See Illustration 35, Tiered Buffet Tables, in this chapter.)

Buffet Servers Although you would think that buffets don't require personal servers, you should place one or two volunteers to oversee each buffet table. If they see someone struggling to balance a plate, glass, and knife, they can lend a helping hand. These servers can keep an eye on what needs to be replenished as well as recite the ingredients of a particular dish for the curious guest. Chop vegetables into convenient sizes; serve raw or marinate and drain. Pre-slice everything; it speeds up serving and allocates fair portions to everyone. Anything in a pie crust is easy to serve.

If you are serving soups or sauces, assign a server to dish these out. A server to carve the lamb or suckling pigs to order is showy but will slow things down. If you opt for this piece of "flash," procure sharp carving equipment and an experienced person. This is no job for a nervous novice with a dull butter knife. Electric knives can make carving much easier for inept people. To keep food costs down, servers should place one or two slices of meat on the guest's platter.

Beverages Designate a separate space or table for beverages and alcohol. This "beverage bar" must be accessible and fit into your traffic pattern. It will be easier to serve this way, easier to clean up, and will allow the bartender to control illegal drinking.

Pretty Tricks Give some thought to the appearance of your buffet. *Never* set your food out in its cooking pots on a bare tabletop. Plan on borrowing (or renting) tablecloths and serving containers. Paper tablecloths are inexpensive and prettier than bare Masonite or Formica, but in a pinch you could also use clean, ironed bedsheets. Lay a narrow mirror "runner" down the center of the table. Tie in with the season: bowls "nesting" in autumn leaves or among mirrors and white fake snow; petals strewn strategically around serving platters; or gift-wrap the whole table with a white sheet and colored ribbons for holiday events.

Take the time to hunt up attractive baskets, bowls, and platters to use as serving dishes. Save or buy sheet cardboard to cover with aluminum foil and use as serving platters or bread plates. Almost any large vegetable or fruit can be hollowed out and used as a container for flowers, candles, or food (carefully match the inside flavor to the outside flavor). Consider having a centerpiece on your buffet table, using an arrangement of flowers or fruit. Do whatever you can to make your tables and food visually appealing.

Placement When the time comes to actually spread out the food, use good logistics and common sense. Food on a slightly crowded, smaller table seems more splendid than the same amount spread over a larger surface, but leave enough room beside dishes for serving purposes. The "start" section of the buffet arrangement should feature the bulky, inexpensive fillers, then place the medium-range items, lastly the meats and expensive side dishes at the "finish" of the buffet.

Label dishes (and list ingredients for exotic creations). This can be done on individual cards placed near the dishes or on a master menu posted nearby. Place condiments and side dishes near the foods they are meant to accompany. If you serve sauces, put small gravy pitchers alongside serving platters. Provide adequate serving utensils; two serving spoons in each large dish will speed serving. Keep back a plate or two of the most popular and expensive foods, such as shrimp and salmon, to serve later.

Maintenance Upkeep is important to the appearance of a buffet table. Take the time to wipe off spills and crumbs and change tablecloths if necessary. Cycle dirty or nearly empty serving platters and clean,

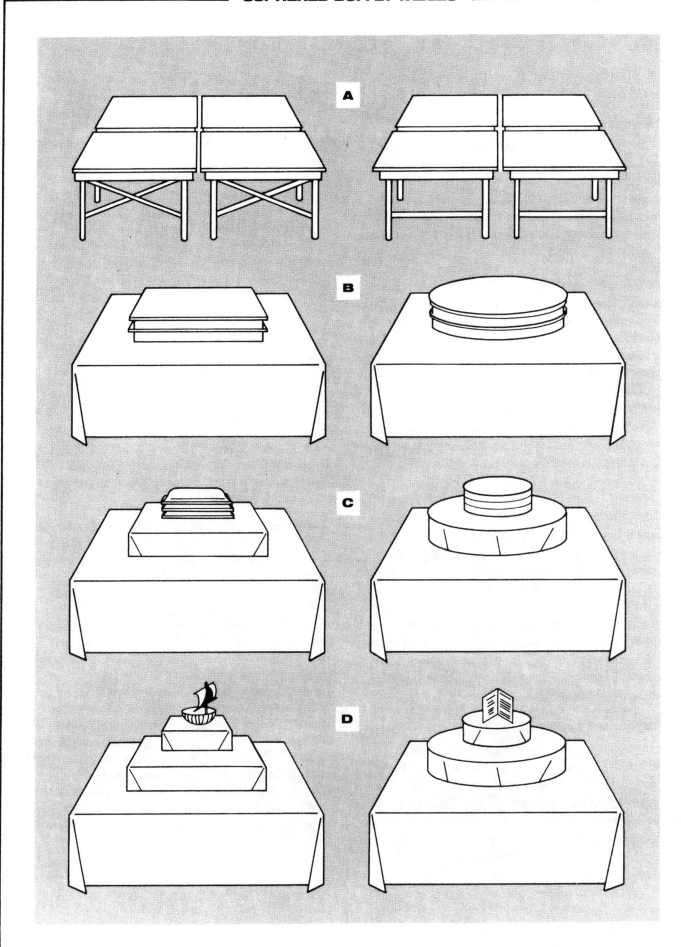

filled platters to the kitchen and back; don't fuss with food while it's on the table.

During the Seated Meal

It's a nice touch to have someone (not necessarily the captain) circle the hall at the beginning of the meal, lighting candles as a gentle signal that the food is about to be served. Call guests to the table about fifteen minutes before you want them to sit down. Dim the lights to soften the atmosphere and encourage conversations; dim light will also make the food look better.

Always serve beverages first, then the rest of the course. Sauces are placed on the table before the item they enhance is served so that guests may combine the two items. For low-budget events, serve more expensive food later in the meal; people will eat less and still appreciate the item.

As the meal proceeds, the captain stands at the passthrough, next to the menu, telling each server the ingredients, portions, and other serving details as the server picks up the food. Each server, in turn, repeats the information to his or her seated guests, if requested.

Shelley Sommer, who organizes special events at the John F. Kennedy Presidential Library and Museum, offers this hint: "The event planner never sits in front for dinner. If the audience sees you getting up and down, they know there's a problem. Sit in the back and let the waiter do the dirty work."

The captain should keep an eye on how portions are distributed. If some tables get extra servings, redistribute them. The captain is also responsible for overseeing the clearing of tables between courses. This is especially important if the kitchen needs the serving dishes for a later course.

Clean as You Go

It makes sense to pay someone else to clean a kitchen. Although friendships are sometimes formed while scrubbing pots, it may be better to hire a teenager. If you rent glassware, dishes, or silverware, find out the cleaning procedures. Some firms want everything rinsed or thoroughly cleaned, others don't.

If you must use your own volunteers, minor upkeep during the preparation of each course will make cleanup faster. Immediately after each stage of preparation is completed, clean as much of that mess as possible before starting the next stage. If the food is being served all at once (as at less formal banquets and buffets), major cleaning begins during the meal; the kitchen will then be under control for the end-of-meal rush. If the meal is served in stages, it will be necessary to clean up as soon as each course is served. Try to set up the kitchen with two tables or windows (one for pickup and one for drop-off) so the next course can be served while cleaning commences on the course just finished. In this way, servers will be able to return dishes from one course and pick up the next course, all in one trip.

It is a good idea to place a supervisor for traffic and garbage control in the drop-off area. The captain can usually be counted on for the part of this function that coincides with the meal. As much as possible, determine in advance which leftovers will be saved and which discarded, and alert those who will handle the returned serving dishes. A crew of three is often best: one to supervise; two to scrape, store, and stack. Rotate volunteers—do not expect the same worker to scrape garbage for two hours.

Leftovers Health regulations may affect your disposal of leftovers. In any case, you can never bring enough Ziplock baggies, aluminum foil, and storage containers. Auction off leftovers or donate them to reward volunteer servers and entertainers. You can also leave manageable-sized packages near the door, marked "Take me home." Try to package nice assortments: a few slices of roast beef, some fruit, a small piece of cheese, rice, and some cookies might appeal to anyone; three gallons of cold rice might not.

Jane McBride Choate of Colorado wrote this idea to *Better Homes and Gardens*: "We had a lot of baked goods left over at the end of our community preschool holiday bazaar. Instead of dividing them up among the workers, we boxed up the goodies and took them to a nearby nursing home. The residents were delighted with the unexpected treat, and we came away with a good feeling." Some groups transport all leftover food to nearby homeless shelters. Flower arrangements can be given to hospitals.

36. SERVING CREW CHECKLIST

Aprons
Dishtowels
Potholders
Can openers
Carts on wheels
Corkscrews and bottle openers
Cutlery
Knives
Ladles
Matches
Pitchers
Plates, bowls, glassware
Serving implements
Serving platters and trays
Spatulas
Warming trays

Menus
Paper
Pens
People place cards
Schedule
Tablecloths and napkins
Table decorations
Table diagrams
Table number cards

37. CLEANUP CREW CHECKLIST

Aprons
Aluminum foil
Brooms
Dishtowels
Dishwashing liquid
Hand soap

Mops and buckets
Paper towels
Sponges
Steel wool
Trash bags
Ziplock bags

RESOURCES

Associations and Agencies

ACCESS: Networking in the Public Interest
Suite 838
1001 Connecticut Ave. NW
Washington, DC 20036-5525
Voice: 202.785.4233
Fax: 202.785.4212
Email: accesscntr@aol.com
URL: http://www.accessjobs.org

American Association of Community Theatre
4712 Enchanted Oaks Dr.
College Station, TX 77845-7649
Voice: 409.774.0611
Fax: 409.776.8718
Email: info@aact.org
URL: http://www.aact.org
Publishes *Spotlight*

American Fund Raising Institute
7004 Comanche Dr.
N. Little Rock, AR 72116-4410
Voice: 800.496.2374
Email: afri@concentric.net
URL: http://www.afri.org

American Program Bureau
36 Crafts St.
Newton, MA 02458-1249
Voice: 800.225.4575
Fax: 617.965.6610
Email: apb@apb-speakers.com
URL: http://www.apb-speakers.com

American Society of Association Executives
1575 I St. NW
Washington, DC 20005-1168
Voice: 202.626.2723
Fax: 202.371.8825
Email: feedback@asaenet.org
URL: http://www.asaenet.org
Publishes *Association Management*

Arts and Business Council Inc.
Suite 702
121 W. 27th St.
New York, NY 10001-6207
Voice: 212.727.7146
Fax: 212.727.3873
Email: info@artsandbusiness.org
URL: http://www.artsandbusiness.org
Publishes *Arts & Business Quarterly*

Association for Volunteer Administration (AVA)
(3108 N. Parham Rd.)
P.O. Box 32092
Richmond, VA 23294-2092
Voice: 804.346.2266
Fax: 804.346.3318

Email: avaintl@mindspring.com
URL: http://www.avaintl.org
Publishes *Journal of Volunteer Administration*

Association for Women in Communications
Suite 6
1244 Ritchie Hwy.
Arnold, MD 21012-1887
Voice: 410.544.7442
Fax: 410.544.4640
URL: http://www.womcom.org
Publishes *The Intercom*

Campus Outreach Opportunity League (COOL)
Suite LL
1531 P St. NW
Washington, DC 20005-1909
Voice: 202.265.1200
Fax: 202.265.3241
Email: homeoffice@COOL2SERVE.org
URL: http://www.cool2serve.org

Catholic Charities USA
Suite 200
1731 King St.
Alexandria, VA 22314-2756
Voice: 703.549.1390
Fax: 703.549.1656
URL: http://www.catholiccharitiesusa.org

Center for Community Change
Suite B
1000 Wisconsin Ave.
Washington, DC 20007-3651
Voice: 202.342.0567
Fax: 202.333.5462
Email: info@communitychange.org
URL: http://www.communitychange.org

Festival Network Online
P.O. Box 18839
Asheville, NC 28814-0839
Voice: 800.200.3737 or 828.658.2779
Email: info@festivalnet.com
URL: http://www.festivalnet.com

GuideStar
Philanthropic Research, Inc.
1126 Professional Dr.
Williamsburg, VA 23185-3330
Voice: 757.229.4631
Fax: 757.229.8912
Email: cstephens@guidestar.org
URL: http://www.guidestar.org

Idealist
Action Without Borders, Inc.
Suite 6614
350 Fifth Ave.
New York, NY 10118-6699

Voice: 212.843.3973
Fax: 212.564.3377
Email: info@idealist.org
URL: www.idealist.org
Publishes *Ideas in Action*

Independent Sector
Suite 200
1200 18th St. NW
Washington, DC 20036-2529
Voice: 202.467.6100
Fax: 202.467.6101
Email: info@indepsec.org
URL: http://www.indepsec.org

Intl. Association of Assembly Managers
(formerly Intl. Association of Auditorium Managers)
Suite 590
4425 W. Airport Freeway
Irving, TX 75062-5835
Voice: 972.255.8020
Fax: 972.255.9582
URL: http://www.iaam.org
Publishes *Facility Manager*

Intl. Association of Conference Centers
243 N. Lindbergh Blvd.
St. Louis, MO 63141-7851
Voice: 314.993.8575
Fax: 314.993.8919
Email: info@iacconline.com
URL: http://www.iacconline.com
Publishes *CenterLines*

Intl. Association of Convention and Visitor Bureaus
(IACVB)
Suite 702
2000 L St. NW
Washington, DC 20036-4990
Voice: 202.296.7888
Fax: 202.296.7889
Email: info@iacvb.org
URL: http://www.iacvb.org/iacvb.html

Intl. Association of Fairs and Expositions
(3043 E. Cairo St.)
P.O. Box 985
Springfield, MO 65801-0985
Voice: 800.516.0313 or 417.862.5771
Fax: 417.862.0156
Email: iafe@iafenet.org
URL: http://www.iafenet.org
Publishes *Fairs and Expos*

Intl. Facilities and Management Association
Suite 1100
1 E. Greenway Plaza
Houston, TX 77046-0194
Voice: 713.623.4362
Fax: 713.623.6124
Email: IFMAhq@ifma.org
URL: http://www.ifma.org

Intl. Festivals & Events Association
(Suite 302, 115 E. Railroad Ave.)
P.O. Box 2950
Port Angeles, WA 98362-0336
Voice: 360.457.3141
Fax: 360.452.4695
URL: http://www.ifea.com
Publishes *Festivals: The How-To of Festivals & Events*

Intl. Society of Meeting Planners
1224 N. Nokomis NE
Alexandria, MN 56308-5072
Voice: 320.763.4919
Fax: 320.763.9290
Email: ismp@iami.org
URL: http://www.iami.org

Intl. Special Events Society (ISES)
Suite 200
9202 N. Meridian St.
Indianapolis, IN 46260-1810
Voice: 317.571.5601 or 800.688.4737
Fax: 317.571.5603
Email: info@ises.com
URL: http://www.ises.com

Intl. TeleConferencing Association
Suite 105
100 Four Falls Corporate Ctr.
W. Conshohocken, PA 19428-2950
Voice: 610.941.2020
Fax: 610.941.2015
Email: info@itca.org
URL: http://www.itca.org

Internet Nonprofit Center
The Evergreen State Society
P.O. Box 20682
Seattle, WA 98102-0682
Voice: 206.329.5640
Fax: 206.322.8348
Email: info@tess.org
URL: http://www.nonprofits.org

Management Assistance Program (MAP) for Nonprofits
Suite 360
2233 University Ave. W.
St. Paul, MN 55114-1629
Voice: 651.647.1216
Fax: 651.647.1369
Email: mail@mapnp.org
URL: http://www.mapnp.org

Meeting Professionals Intl. (MPI)
(formerly Meeting Planners Intl.)
Suite 1200
4455 LBJ Freeway
Dallas, TX 75244-5903
Voice: 972.702.3000
Fax: 972.702.3070
Email: membership@mpiweb.org
URL: http://www.mpiweb.org
Publishes *The Meeting Professional*

Museum Trustee Association
Suite 330
1200 19th St. NW
Washington, DC 20036-2422
Voice: 202.857.1180
Fax: 202.223.4579
URL: http://www.mta-hq.org
Publishes *Museum Trusteeship*

National Association for Campus Activities (NACA)
13 Harbison Way
Columbia, SC 29212-3401
Voice: 803.732.6222
URL: http://www.naca.org
Publishes *Campus Activities Programming*

National Association of Catering Executives (NACE)
Suite 328
5565 Sterrett Pl.
Columbia, MD 21044-2684
Voice: 410.997.9055
Fax: 410.997.8834
URL: http://www.nace.net

National Association for the Exchange of Industrial
Resources (NAEIR)
560 McClure St.
Galesburg, IL 61401-4286
Voice: 800.562.0955
Fax: 309.343.0862
Email: donor@naeir.org
URL: http://www.freegoods.com

National Association of Sports Officials (NASO)
2017 Lathrop Ave.
Racine, WI 53405-3755
Voice: 414.632.5448
Fax: 414.632.5460
Email: cservice@naso.org
URL: http://www.naso.org
Publishes *It's Official*

National Association of Town Watch (NATW)
P.O. Box 303
Wynnewood, PA 19096-0303
Voice: 610.649.7055
Email: NATWNNO@aol.com
URL: http://www.nationaltownwatch.org
Publishes *New Spirit*

National Charities Information Bureau (NCIB)
Sixth Floor
19 Union Square W.
New York, NY 10003-3395
Voice: 212.929.6300
Fax: 212.463.7083
URL: http://www.give.org

National Society of Fund-Raising Executives
NSFRE Fund-Raising Resource Center
Suite 700
1101 King St.
Alexandria, VA 22314-2967

Voice: 703.684.0410
Fax: 703.684.0540
Email: nsfre@nsfre.org
URL: http://www.nsfre.org
Publishes *Advancing Philanthropy*

National Speakers Association
Suite 101
1500 S. Priest Dr.
Tempe, AZ 85281-6266
Voice: 602.968.2552
Fax: 602.968.0911
Email: Information@nsaspeaker.org
URL: http://www.nsaspeaker.org
Publishes *Professional Speaker*

Philanthropic Advisory Service
Council of Better Business Bureaus
Suite 800
4200 Wilson Blvd.
Arlington, VA 22203-1838
Email: bbb@bbb.org
URL: http://www.bbb.org
Publishes *Give But Give Wisely*

Points of Light Foundation
Suite 800
1400 I St. NW
Washington, DC 20005-6526
Voice: 202.729.8000
Fax: 202.729.8100
Email: volnet@pointsoflight.org
URL: http://www.pointsoflight.org
Publishes *Leadership*

Professional Convention Management Association
Suite 220
100 Vestavia Pkwy.
Birmingham, AL 35216-3781
Voice: 205.823.7262
Fax: 205.822.3891
URL: http://www.pcma.org
Publishes *Convene*

Public Relations Society of America (PRSA)
33 Irving Pl.
New York, NY 10003-2376
Voice: 212.995.2230
Email: hq@prsa.org
URL: http://www.prsa.org
Publishes *Tactics*

Religious Conference Management Association (RCMA)
Suite 120
One RCA Dome
Indianapolis, IN 46225-1023
Voice: 317.632.1888
Fax: 317.632.7909
URL: http://www.rcmaweb.org
Publishes *Religious Conference Manager*

Society of Government Meeting Professionals (SGMP)
6 Clouser Rd.
Mechanicsburg, PA 17055-9735
Voice: 717.795.7467
Fax: 717.795.7473
URL: http://www.sgmp.org

Society for Nonprofit Organizations
Suite 1
6314 Odana Rd.
Madison, WI 53719-1141
Voice: 608.274.9777
Fax: 608.274.9978
Email: snpo@danenet.wicip.org
URL: http://danenet.wicip.org/snpo
Publishes *Nonprofit World*

Support Center for Nonprofit Management
Fifth Floor
706 Mission St.
San Francisco, CA 94103-3113
Voice: 415.541.9000
Fax: 415.541.7708
Email: supportcenter@supportcenter.org
URL: www.supportcenter.org
Publishes *Board Café*

Toastmasters Intl.
P.O. Box 9052
Mission Viejo, CA 92690-9052
Voice: 949.858.8255
Fax: 949.858.1207
Email: tminfo@toastmasters.org
URL: http://www.toastmasters.org
Publishes *The Toastmaster*

United Way of America
701 N. Fairfax St.
Alexandria, VA 22314-2045
Voice: 703.836.7100
Fax: 703.683.7811
URL: http://www.unitedway.org
Publishes *Community*

Catalogs, On-line Directories, and Miscellaneous

ARDI Resource Directory
Applied Research & Development Intl., Inc.
Suite 311, Bevans Bldg.
6740 E. Hampden Ave.
Denver, CO 80224-3019
Voice: 303.691.6076
Fax: 303.691.6077
Email: ardibw@aol.com
URL: http://www.ardi.org

Badge A Minit
P.O. Box 800
LaSalle, IL 61301-0800
Voice: 800.223.4103
Fax: 815.883.9696
Email: questions@badgeaminit.com

URL: http://www.badgeaminit.com

Charity Village
P.O. Box 92536
160 Main St. S.
Brampton, Ontario
Canada, L6W 4R1
Voice: 905.453.7321
Fax: 905.456.9729
Email: help@charityvillage.com
URL: http://www.charityvillage.com

CyberVPM.com
9594 First Ave. NE # 413
Seattle, WA 98115-2012
Voice: 206.525.2104
Fax: 206.525.3320
Email: info@cybervpm.com
URL: www.cybervpm.com

EventSource.com
Suite 115
480 Gate Five Rd.
Sausalito, CA 94965-1461
Voice: 415.883.9100
Fax: 415.883.8239
Email: support@eventsource.com
URL: http://eventsource.com

Festival
RSL Interactive
1001 Alaskan Way
Pier 55, Suite 288
Seattle, WA 98101-1028
Voice: 206.623.9495
Fax: 206.623.8002
Email: alliances@rslinteractive.com
URL: http://www.festivals.com

Harrah College of Hotel Administration
University of Nevada, Las Vegas
4505 Maryland Pkwy.
P.O. Box 456013
Las Vegas, NV 89154-6013
Voice: 702.895.3161
Fax: 702.895.4109
URL: http://www.unlv.edu/Colleges/Hotel

Meeting Industry Mall
Email: webmaster@mim.com
URL: http://www.mim.com

MeetingsNet
Adams Business Media/Meetings Group
68-860 Perez Rd.
Cathedral City, CA 92234-7249
Voice: 760.770.4370
Fax: 760.770.5868
Email: mtgmgr@meetingsnet.com
URL: http://www.meetingsnet.com
Publishes *Corporate Meetings & Incentives* and
Association Meetings

National Volunteer Week Catalog
Great Events Publishing
135 Dupont St.
P.O. Box 760
Plainview, NY 11803-0760
Voice: 888.433.8386
Fax: 516.349.5521

Smart Business Supersites
8 Orchard Cir. # CN5219
Princeton, NJ 08540-3026
Fax: 732.321.5156
Email: editor@smartbiz.com
URL: http://www.smartbiz.com

The Taft Group
27500 Drake Rd.
Farmington Hills, MI 48331-3535
Voice: 800.877.TAFT
Fax: 800.414.5043
Email: referencedesk@gale.com
URL: http://www.taftgroup.com

TS Central
149 Cedar St.
Wellesley, MA 02481-5504
Voice: 781.235.8095
Fax: 781.416.4500
Email: info@tscentral.com
URL: http://ww0.tscentral.com

Volunteer Energy
Energize, Inc.
Suite C1
5450 Wissahickon Ave.
Philadelphia, PA 19144-5292
Voice: 215.438.8342
Fax: 215.438.0434
Email: info@energizeinc.com
URL: http://www.energizeinc.com

Volunteer Marketplace Catalog
See Points of Light Foundation

Publications

Association Meetings
See *MeetingsNet*

Chase's Calendar of Events: The Day-By-Day Directory to Special Days, Weeks and Months
Contemporary Books (annual)

Chicago Special Events Sourcebook: The Comprehensive Guide to Great Locations in Chicago and Suburbs for Meetings, Parties, Weddings
Editor: Melissa Derkacz
Independent Publishers Group, 1998

Contributions
P.O. Box 338
Medfield, MA 02052-0338
Voice: 508.359.0019

Fax: 508.359.8084
Email: contrib@ziplink.net
URL: http://www.contributionsmagazine.com
Corporate Meetings & Incentives
See *MeetingsNet*

Event Web Newsletter
Doug Fox Communications
11817 Chase Wellesley Dr. #927
Richmond, VA 23233-7765
Voice: 804.364.1212
Fax: 804.749.3076
Email: dougfox@eventweb.com
URL: http://www.eventweb.com

Fund$raiser Cyberzine
12101 Seven Mile Rd. NE
Belding, MI 48809-9617
Voice: 616.691.7574
Fax: 616.691.8079
Email: brengled@fundsraiser.com
URL: http://www.fundsraiser.com

The Fundraiser's Guide
Arkansas Support Network
P.O. Box 697
Bentonville, AR 72712-0697
Voice: 501.273.0338
Fax: 501.271.0819
Email: fssi@ipa.net
URL: http://www.fundraisers-guide.com

Grapevine: Volunteerism's Newsletter
Editor: Susan Vineyard
1807 Prairie Ave.
Downers Grove, IL 60515-3314
Voice: 630.964.1194
Fax: 630.964.7338
Email: vineyards1@aol.com

Grassroots Fundraising Journal
Chardon Press
3781 Broadway
Oakland, CA 94611-5613
Voice: 510.596.8160
Fax: 510.596.8822
Email: chardon@chardonpress.com
URL: http://www.chardonpress.com

The Guide to Unique Meeting & Event Facilities
Amarc, Inc.
P.O. Box 279
Minturn, CO 81645-0279
Voice: 970.827.5500
Fax: 970.827.9411
Email: email@theguide.com
URL: http://www.theguide.com

Meetings and Conventions Magazine
8773 S. Ridgeline Blvd.
Highlands Ranch, CO 80126-7500
Voice: 800.446.6551
Fax: 303.470.4546

Email: cahners.subs@denver.cahners.com
URL: http://www.meetings-conventions.com

Mid-Atlantic Events Magazine
Suite 700
1080 N. Delaware Ave.
Philadelphia, PA 19125-4330
Voice: 215.426.7800
Fax: 215.426.9720
Email: editor@eventsmagazine.com
URL: http://www.eventsmagazine.com

New England Nonprofit Quarterly
Suite 700
18 Tremont St.
Boston, MA 02108-2307
Voice: 617.523.6565
Fax: 617.523.2070
Email: editor@newenglandnonprofit.org
URL: http://www.newenglandnonprofit.org

Nonprofit Issues, Inc.
P.O. Box 482
Dresher, PA 19025-0482
Voice: 215.542.7547
Fax: 215.542.7548
Email: info@nonprofitissues.com
URL: http://www.nonprofitissues.com

Non-Profit Nuts & Bolts
4623 Tiffany Woods Circle
Oviedo, FL 32765-6102
Voice: 407.677.6564
Fax: 407.677.5645
Email: info@nutsbolts.com
URL: http://www.nutsbolts.com

Nonprofit Online News
The Gilbert Center
400 Harvard Ave. E. #211
Seattle, WA 98102-4951
Email: info@gilbert.org
URL: http://www.gilbert.org/news

The NonProfit Times
Suite 318
240 Cedar Knolls Rd.
Cedar Knolls, NJ 07927-1626
Voice: 973.734.1700
Fax: 973.734.1777
Email: ednchief@nptimes.com
URL: http://www.nptimes.com

Philanthropy News Network Online
Suite 805, Raleigh Bldg.
5 W. Hargett St.
Raleigh, NC 27601-1348
Voice: 919.832.2325
Fax: 919.832.2369
Email: pnninfo@mindspring.com
URL: http://www.pj.org

Special Events Magazine
(23815 Stuart Ranch Rd.)
P.O. Box 8987
Malibu, CA 90265-8987
Voice: 310.317.4522 or 800.543.4116
Fax: 310.317.9644
URL: http://www.specialevents.com/magazine

Student Leader
Oxendine Publishing, Inc.
P.O. Box 14081
Gainesville, FL 32604-2081
Voice: 352.373.6907
Fax: 352.373.8120
URL: http://www.studentleader.com

Successful Meetings Magazine
355 Park Ave. S.
New York, NY 10010-1789
Voice: 212.592.6403
Fax: 212.592.6409
URL: http://www.successmtgs.com

Sunshine Artist Magazine
2600 Temple Dr.
Winter Park, FL 32789-1371
Voice: 407.539.1399
Fax: 407.539.1499
Email: editor@sunshineartist.com
URL: http://www.sunshineartist.com

The Teacher's Calendar 1999-2000: The Day-By-Day Directory of Holidays, Historic Events, Birthdays and Special Days, Weeks and Months
Authors: Sandra Whiteley, Kim Summers, Sally M. Walker
Contemporary Books, 1999

Volunteer Management Report
Stevenson Consultants, Inc.
(417 Eton Ct.)
P.O. Box 4528
Sioux City, IA 51104-4528
Voice: 712.239.3010
Fax: 712.239.2166

The Volunteer's Survival Manual: The Only Practical Guide to Giving Your Time & Money
Author: Darcy Campion Devney
The Practical Press, 1992

Volunteer Today: The Electronic Gazette for Volunteerism
MBA Publishing
821 Lincoln St.
Walla Walla, WA 99362-3235
Voice: 509.529.0244
Fax: 509.529.8865
Email: mba@bmi.net
URL: http://www.volunteertoday.com

INDEX

Here are some other books on similar topics from Pineapple Press. For a complete catalog, write to Pineapple Press, P.O. Box 3889, Sarasota, Florida 34230-3889, or call (800) 746-3275. Or visit our website at www.pineapplepress.com.

The Business of Special Events by Harry A. Freedman and Karen Feldman. Successful nonprofit managers know that to raise money for their cause they must approach fundraising as if it were a for-profit business. This how-to covers every aspect of producing profitable special events, from sidewalk sales to glamorous galas. ISBN 1-56164-141-3 (pb)

The Club Board Members Guide by John L. Carroll. Although written with private club members in mind, the common-sense solutions offered here apply to a much broader audience, especially those who oversee the running of a nonprofit organization. Having served on many club boards, usually as president, John Carroll shows how a fine-tuned sense of "people skills," coupled with an understanding of how every organization functions, creates an atmosphere where decisions can be made for the benefit of the club and its members. Learn what to expect as a club board member: How do you communicate effectively with your members and the public? What are your legal responsibilities? How should meetings be handled? What about issues of money? ISBN 1-56164-244-4 (pb)

Games for Fundraising by William N. Czuckrey Who doesn't love a fair? The barker's cry, "Step right up, ladies and gentlemen!," the sound of hoops clattering over pegs and balls hitting their targets, the colorful booths, the mysterious fortune-tellers—all contribute to the excitement and fun of trying your luck or skill to win a prize. And it all adds up to substantial profits for the sponsoring organization. For anyone who is faced with the challenge of creating an exciting special event to raise funds with games, this book offers a selection of games sure to delight all ages, complete with step-by-step instructions. ISBN 1-56164-074-3 (pb)

Keep the Money Coming by Christine Graham. Every nonprofit organization needs to find a reliable way to fund the budget—every year. This book offers nonprofit organizations the basic skills for annual fundraising. You will find powerful tools, sage advice, and proven methods to help you raise the money your organization needs every year. According to Christine Graham: "Half your job is to learn how to raise money and the other half will be to get yourselves to do it." This book helps on both counts! ISBN 1-56164-025-5 (pb)

A Primer on Nonprofit PR: If Charity Begins at Home . . . by Kathleen A. Neal. Drawing on her thirty years of experience, Kathleen Neal defines public relations and then shows how it can be used creatively and effectively for nonprofit organizations. This book is chock full of ideas and strategies for applying solid PR techniques to the nonprofit, often accompanied by personal accounts of successful (and not so successful) PR efforts described with insight and a wry sense of humor. Plan a fundraising event, deal with a crisis, defuse a tense situation, develop a relationship with the media, and all the while promote your organization, keeping its mission in the eye of the public. Let this book be your how-to manual for a successful public relations program. ISBN 1-56164-229-0 (pb)